The Navajos Are Coming To Jesus

by
Thomas Dolaghan
David Scates

William Carey Library
533 HERMOSA STREET • SOUTH PASADENA, CALIF. 91030

Library of Congress Cataloging in Publication Data

Scates, David R   1932–
   The Navajos are coming to Jesus.

   Bibliography: p.
   1. Navaho Indians—Missions. 2. Indians of North
America—Southwest, New—Missions. 3. Navaho Indians—
Religion and mythology. 4. Indians of North America—
Southwest, New—Religion and mythology. 5. Christianity
—Southwest, New. I. Dolaghan, Thomas, 1927–
joint author. II. Title.
E99.N3S32   280'.4'097913   78-3609
ISBN 0-87808-162-3

Published by the William Carey Library
533 Hermosa Street
South Pasadena, California 91030
Telephone (213) 798-0819

In accord with some of the most recent thinking in the academic
press, the William Carey Library is pleased to present this
scholarly book which has been prepared from an author-edited
and author-prepared camera ready copy.

PRINTED IN THE UNITED STATES OF AMERICA

Contents

Foreword

Current information about the American Indian Christian community, the local churches, the pastors, the mission agencies, and the trends in life and ministry is woefully lacking. There is general awareness of a crisis in ministry. There is not enough knowledge to produce a basis for study, reflection, and action. Tom Dollaghan and David Scates have made a survey which provides accurate data about the churches on the Navajo Reservation. It is hoped that their work will inspire others to do the same sort of investigation in other reservations and regions.

Moreover, this survey gives cause to praise and thank the Lord. It reveals a great movement of the Holy Spirit in Navajo land and an amazing development of indigenous leadership and congregations. The authors provide a factual basis for united and individual planning and action. They give missionaries reason for sober reflection and Navajo pastors cause for encouragement. This study can be expected to lift hearts, inspire renewed dedication, and strengthen further evangelistic witness and pastoral care. It may give hope to pastors and workers among other Native American peoples also.

R. Pierce Beaver

Preface

Here is a document of great significance for
both missiology and anthropology. It is a patient
piece of research which involved Scates and Dolaghan
in visiting every corner of the Navajo Reservation.
With remarkable skill and empathy they established
rapport with all kinds of Navajo. They joined in
their worship, ate their food, attended their camp
meetings, and spent hours conversing in the Navajo
language. Thus they picked up leads about pockets
of Navajo Christians in remote places, and they
followed up those leads with patient persistence.
I have seen these men at work and know well the wide
range of Navajo contacts they have established, and
the character of their participant interaction in
Navajo groups.

Exploring an old mission field which has been
very resistant to the gospel, they have discovered
how the Navajo church can grow where the evangelism
is done by Navajo evangelists, and the dynamics of
their acceptance of the gospel. This is intensely
important for the strategy of mission.

Anthropologically they have given us a full
synchronic study of spacial diffusion through a system of micro-regions. Quite apart from the valuable
missiological information it contains, this work is
an extremely important document for the development
of a methodology for charting religious change.

I recommend this book to all persons interested
in the dynamics of religious change whether their
interests be either missionary or academic. It is a
most significant study.

                                    Alan R. Tippett

Introduction

This study is a result of an informal meeting of the authors in the patio at Fuller Seminary where we both were students at the School of World Mission. From the background of a combined 24 years of service on the Navajo field, we were asking how the Navajo people could most effectively be evangelized. It became obvious as we struggled with this question that we needed more information. We needed to know something of the strength and character of the Protestant churches. We also needed to know if we were in a period of growth or decline, which would give us an idea of the receptivity of the people to the Gospel. The growth of individual churches and denominations needed to be studied to gain insights as to what methodology or emphasis was producing optimum results. Plans were laid and the survey was begun at the end of June, 1976.

Our methodology for this study included visiting on location almost all churches on the Navajo Reservation. We used a simple form to gather information.

We divided the Reservation down the middle, but much of our survey was done together. We spent from one to two weeks each month visiting churches. We both are fluent enough in Navajo to conduct our interviews in English or Navajo. Often there were no English speaking people available. We enjoyed interviewing a broad spectrum of missionaries, pastors, lay workers and church members.

Often no one knew we were coming and we did not

know where we were going; we had no advance way of
knowing where churches were located, so we found
people exactly as they normally would be. We would
take one area at a time, travel the main road until
we found a Navajo home and begin asking what churches were in the area. The more we scratched, the
more we uncovered. At every church we would ask
"Are there any other churches around here?" When we
were getting the same answers from everyone we
talked to, we suspected we had found all the congregations in that area.

We interviewed missionaries, pastors, lay workers and church members in 249 different congregations. We attended one or more services in 55 of
these congregations. Information from another 81
churches was gathered from individuals well acquainted with these churches. Additional information was
gathered from questionnaires sent out to the churches.

We were well received in all but two or three
homes out of the 300-400 that we visited. Some
were suspicious of our intent at first, but more
often than not we spent an hour or two at each
place and found it hard to leave. Rapport often
came because we could converse in Navajo. At times
we were asked to stay or come back and preach. It
was difficult to refuse. We stayed in commodious
mission accommodations and slept on occasion in
Navajo homes. We stayed where invited, and were
often invited to stay.

Our conversation would begin in either Navajo
or English by telling them who we were, where we
were from, and stating our business in broad terms,
such as, "We are doing a survey of all the congregations on the Reservation to learn how many congregations there are, how many Navajos are attending church and what the Lord is doing in each
area."

We were then usually invited into the home.
After a few minutes of letting them volunteer information about their church or mission we then
would ask about their times of services, average
attendance, attendance at other services, how many
children, how many women, how many men, how many

Anglos, how many Sunday school classes, teachers, etc. We would always ask what they had found to be the most effective means of evangelism. We would ask what other services the mission provided, and how long the mission or congregation had been there. We asked about offerings, whether services were in Navajo or English, and the name and address of the pastor. We were never in a hurry and found most missionaries and pastors starved for fellowship. We liked to close our interview with prayer for that congregation and for the evangelization of the Navajo people.

EXTENT AND LIMITATIONS OF THE SURVEY

The survey covered every one of the 23 districts except District 6, which is the Hopi Reservation, and District 20 which, for some reason, does not exist (see District maps). Also covered in the survey were Districts 21, 22 and 23 which are separate small reservations isolated geographically from the rest of the Navajo Reservation and all border towns that are adjacent to the Reservation (see maps). Navajos living in large urban areas such as Los Angeles, Albuquerque, Phoenix, Denver, etc. were not covered. The survey was made of all Protestant churches and congregations. We interviewed missionaries, pastors, lay workers and church members in 249 different congregations, and attended one or more services in 55 of these congregations. Information from another 81 churches was gathered from individuals well acquainted with these churches. Additional information was gathered from questionnaires, sent out to the churches. We did not survey the 31 Roman Catholic churches and chapels, or the 15-20 Latter Day Saints churches, although we had enjoyable and profitable visits with some of these congregations. We plan to update this survey in the not too distant future and we will include these churches in an appendix. The survey focused on congregations rather than support agencies. Anglo missionaries and mission staff workers are not included in our statistics, except where an Anglo is pastoring a congregation. While it was

not a church growth survey in the classical McGavran
sense, it was an attempt to look at the present state
of churches and the extent to which Navajos have been
evangelized and incorporated into them.

The reason for the publication of this study is
to provide information that will give missionaries,
pastors and mission boards an accurate picture of the
church among the Navajo today. As we become aware of
the strength of the churches, the resources available
in terms of potential leadership and Christian workers and the receptivity of the people, we can then
pray and plan more intelligently.

The brief overview of Navajo history, social
structure and religion is given for the benefit of
new missionaries and those unfamiliar with the Navajo
people.   The bibliography contains a number of
sources that should be helpful to the serious
student.   It is our firm conviction that the cross-
cultural worker must understand the people in order
to minister effectively to them.

In Part II we answer the questions of when and
where Navajos began coming to Jesus. It is important
that we analyze the different church structures and
mission approaches to evangelism in order to gain insights that will be of value to us in the future. The
historical sketch of missions is intended to give
"time depth" to our perception of the progress of
Christianity in Navajoland. From this perspective
it should be obvious that God is giving us a time of
receptivity, an "open door" for the evangelism of the
people. Finally, we deal with how Navajos are coming
to Jesus. Here we try to focus on some factors that
must be taken into consideration if we are to hone
the cutting edge of our evangelistic strategy.   In
these articles we attempt to deal with the kind of
communication of the Gospel that results in the
growth of the church. We then take a look at the dynamics of Navajo conversions when allowed to take
place by family groups with the least possible social
dislocation, rather than one by one against the social tide. All in all, we have found Jesus' hand at
work in building His Church among the Navajo people
producing quality Christians, sometimes in the least
likely places, but always bearing the fruit of the

Spirit. To be among these Christians was reward enough for the project.

In conclusion, we would like to express our thanks to our two boards [1] for allowing us the time and finances to carry out this survey. It is a tribute to their breadth of vision for the work of God among the Navajo people. We would also like to express our sincere appreciation to all missionaries and pastors who were so cooperative and hospitable. We were received with warmth and courtesy everywhere we went. The ripening harvest that is evident today is the result of many years of faithful sowing by dedicated servants of God. Our sincere prayer is that God will enable us all to lift up our eyes, see the field and by His power and for His glory reap an abundant harvest.

NOTES

1) Tom Dolaghan works with Navajo Gospel Mission and David Scates is with Navajo Christian Churches.

Acknowledgments

We would like to give special recognition to Linda Wisdom for her help in organizing the data gathered from the survey. In addition to this, she spent many hours in typing the manuscripts and in the preparation of charts and maps.

We also wish to thank Mr. and Mrs. Warren Davis for proof reading and for their many helpful suggestions.

We are both indebted to Dr. Tippett, our mentor at the School of World Mission at Fuller Seminary,for the encouragement to undertake this project.

We would be remiss if we failed to recognize the help given by our wives, Betty Dolaghan and Peggy Scates, not only in reading, typing and helpful criticism but for their wholehearted encouragement and support during the year this study was in process.

Part One

The Navajos

1
The Navajos Today

The Navajo Nation, as the people proudly call themselves today, occupies a reservation covering 25,000 square miles in Arizona, Utah and New Mexico. The estimated population on the Reservation is over 160,000 and the Navajo growth rate is twice that of the United States population as a whole. (Terrell 1972: IV) Navajos have been referred to as the fastest growing ethnic group in the United States. The Navajos are part of a linguistic group known as Athabascan, which includes tribes in Canada, Alaska, the northwestern United States and the Southwest, including the Apaches.

The Navajo people are making rapid progress under the leadership of their tribal chairman, Peter MacDonald, and a council made up of representatives from the twenty-one districts. They have their own system of law enforcement and courts aided by the FBI which deals with major crimes. Education for all children, industry, and the pick-up truck all contribute to acculturation toward the dominant Anglo society. The pace would be much faster were it not for the strength of the Navajo social system and traditional way of life.

THE NAVAJO SOCIAL STRUCTURE

The nuclear family consists of a man, his wife, and his unmarried children. It is the smallest viable economic and residence group in Navajo society. The members eat, sleep and live together in the same

hoghan. As a group, the nuclear family is responsible
for economic support and the rearing of the children.
Traditionally, it is attached at the outset to an extended family, preferably, but not invariably that of
the bride. Later, the nuclear family may break off
and establish its own camp, but this is not done
until the couple has enough livestock and enough man-
power to be self-sustaining.

The extended family is a group based on kinship,
co-residence and cooperation that typically comprises
three generations: grandparents, parents and children. It is composed of at least two nuclear families affiliated through the extension of the parent-
child relationship with each living in its own hoghan
"within shouting distance of each other." Each member of the extended family is expected to contribute
work, sheep or money to common enterprises and, con-
versely, expects aid from the group in paying a debt,
in holding a sing or in providing the goods that are
customarily demanded as a bride price. The extended
family offers security to individuals who have left
the group but who are free to return in case of unem-
ployment, divorce or death of a spouse.

Authority is exercised with a great deal of
flexibility. The principal responsibility for organizing joint efforts rests upon the oldest able-
bodied man. In some cases an older woman might take
this position. The amount of authority depends upon
the personality of the person who takes the lead.
This authority is not coercive, however. The leader
can only plan, advise and ask for cooperation. Things
are talked over by the adult members of the extended
family (camp).

Nuclear families periodically move to a new
location and begin a new camp in order to find enough
grazing for their sheep. This will not be more than
a few miles away from the parent camp and for this
reason there are usually a number of related camps in
an area. The majority of camps are matrilocal, a few
being patrilocal or neolocal.

Navajos trace their lineage through the mother -
they are "born for" their father. The Navajo matri-
lineage never meets as a decision-making group, nor
does it wield authority as a unit,but the obligations

for mutual help are upon the members of that lineage.
Land and water use is all regulated by the members of
the lineage and not by the larger clan relationship.
The clan is the largest consanguineous kinship
group whose members acknowledge a traditional bond of
common descent in the maternal line. Clan membership
serves to regulate marriage and provides a widespread
network for hospitality. While one is a member of
his mother's clan, it is also common to mention the
father's clan and thus open up a wider range of cooperation and aid. In times of need, however, a husband
will go to members of his mother's lineage and a wife
to hers. Clans are exogamic, named, matrilineal and
dispersed. (Shephardson-Hammond 1970:44,45).
The Navajo Reservation is divided into districts. Each district has a chapter house where meetings are held to discuss decisions made by the Tribal
Council at Window Rock and matters relating to the
area such as work projects and distribution of surplus commodities. A delegate is chosen from each
area to serve on the Tribal Council. Each chapter
house has also a president, secretary and treasurer.
Most of these officers are men and, again, the leadership is not coercive but seeks the mind of the
group. The Tribal Council is the governing body for
the Tribe.

Paired Roles (Dyads)
The principal role system in Navajo society according to Shephardson and Hammond is the interrela-
tion of kinship roles. It is important that the
missionary be aware of these in order to understand
who might be the most likely innovators and leaders.
This subject is too extensive for us to pursue in
this article, but it would be safe to generalize that
communication takes place rather easily between kin
relatives. The closest relationships are husband-
wife, mother-child, maternal grandmother-daughter's
child, mother's brother/sister's child and that between siblings. Affinal relationships is a very sen-
sitive area, especially that of mother-in-law to son-
in-law, which includes avoidance with the sanction of
possible blindness. In *Navajo Mountain Community*,
Shephardson and Hammond have an excellent discussion
of these paired relationships (1970:66-98). These

institutionalized patterns of communication which include teasing,   joking,   etc.,   allow us to   pinpoint
channels of communication.   As will be seen in a study of the Black Mesa Church and in many other   Navajo
churches, kin lines provide bridges for   proclamation
and persuasion.

Culture Change
     Within the past twenty years, the rate of change
in the Navajo culture has been accelerating.   During
the past 12-15 years almost all Navajo children   have
been enrolled in school.   Schooling is   primarily in
the English language using Anglo-oriented textbooks.[1]
With the increase of available jobs and more recently
welfare,   more of the people   have pick-up trucks and
so have   become   much more aware   of life outside the
Reservation.   Rectangular houses built with aid   from
Tribal funds are slowly replacing the traditional hoghans.   Canned goods   are being added   to   the staple
diet in many homes   and   the style of clothing is becoming that   of the   dominant culture.   While   some
women still   weave rugs,   this occupation   is   not as
prevalent because   of the availability   of cash from
other sources.   The manufacture of turquoise jewelry,
however, has increased because of popular demand   and
high prices.
     While the religion   is still that   of the tradi-
tional culture   and   the   Peyote nativistic movement,
more and more of the young people seem less   informed
or interested in either.   They are still loyal to the
family, however, and attend ceremonies   which provide
a good   social function.   Many of them laugh   at the
idea of witchcraft,   but   seem to be   less than   convinced that it is merely fiction.   This, however,   is
a different attitude   than that   of their parents who
are   very much afraid   of witchcraft   and would never
joke about it.
     Perhaps   the most   significant change   in Navajo
society is   the development   of the   semi-urban mixed
community.   This type   of community   is growing   up
around government boarding schools and hospitals. The
Tribal government   has insisted   that   these institutions employ Navajos for every position that they are
capable of filling.   Modern housing   is provided for

the workers with running water and electricity.
Other enterprising Navajos have opened up businesses
to provide services for these well-paid workers. As
a result of this, more houses are built in the community or mobile homes are brought in. This is becoming "the good life" in Navajoland and these jobs are
much sought after. The younger adults enjoy the modern conveniences and gadgets as well as television
and community movies. One of their biggest problems
is keeping the other family members from moving in
with them. This life-style is preferred to the off-
reservation life of the urban Indian. Here it is
possible to enjoy the best of both worlds. One has
the security of being on home ground and attending
traditional functions and, at the same time, enjoying
many of the benefits of the white man's way of life.
These people are predisposed to change and we believe
they are the most receptive segment of Navajo society
to the Gospel.

The Urban Navajo

Let us now look at one other segment of Navajo
society, the people who, for the most part out of
necessity, have moved to the large cities. We will
refer to these people as urban Navajo. There are
some eight to ten thousand of these people in Los
Angeles County alone. Other significant groups are
in Chicago, Denver, Dallas, San Francisco and
Albuquerque. Our information about these people will
be taken from a study done in Albuquerque by William
H. Hodge (1969). Hodge points out that those who
are permanent residents in the city are those who
have made the transition and have become acculturated. Their children often do not speak Navajo and
their visits to the Reservation are infrequent, perhaps once a year to visit relatives. These people,
however, are in the minority. Most urban Navajo
have a strong attraction to the Reservation and their
aim is to return there when it is possible to make an
adequate living. They would prefer to live in one of
the semi-urban communities on the Reservation because
they find the modern conveniences in the city desir-
able. These people are highly mobile, being disillu-
sioned in turn with both city and reservation life.

The pull toward the Reservation is due to con-
genial family ties, a more relaxed atmosphere, language barriers, inability to make a living, unful-
filled obligations to reservation kinsmen and an inability to cope with city life, stress, etc. There is
often a problem with liquor resulting in the loss of
a job, mounting bills and trouble with the law. When
on the Reservation, the pull toward the city is due
to job opportunity, escape from unsatisfying reservation life, higher standard of living, good medical
care, language barriers for the children who don't
speak Navajo and boredom.

These different stages of acculturation will be
referred to in other chapters since they must be
taken into consideration if we are to have an effective ministry to the Navajo people.

NAVAJO RELIGION

All we will endeavor to do here is to make a few
remarks about the nature of Navajo religion. The
reader can refer to the bibliography for books that
deal with this subject in depth. What is given may
be of help to the missionary who is working with
people other than Navajos and who is interested in
church growth in the Navajo context.

The Navajo does not have a systematized religion
with a set form of worship, a body of doctrine or a
code of ethics. In fact, the spiritual forces that
control or influence the affairs of humans are not
thought of as supernatural; they are simply part of
the cosmos. While some of the younger people might
talk about "our" religion, it is simply an attempt to
identify the spiritual dimension of their culture in
a way that makes sense to outsiders. "The Navajo Way"
is an expression that is used by most of the people
and includes the totality of life; spiritual and
material. The Navajos would not even recognize this
dichotomy, however.

The origin myths which vary with different
versions tell of the first world in which mist beings
dwelt. Through various events (mishaps or infractions of accepted behavior) they moved through several worlds with each world and its inhabitants becoming part of the next world. These dieties (Holy

People) seem to be the prototypes of human and animal life which live on earth today and are called by their present names. The Holy People entered this world (the glittering world) having been flooded out of the previous by Water Monster whose baby had been stolen by the rascal Coyote. "The Place Where They Emerged" *(Hajiinei)* is pointed out today as a spot covered by Navajo Lake in northwest New Mexico. First Man and First Woman formed the four sacred mountains that surround Navajoland.

Other stories explain the origin of the world of nature and man's place in it, e.g., the story of the twin heros, Monster Slayer and Child Born of the Water. Their mother, Changing Woman, is perhaps the best known diety to Navajos. They journeyed in search of their father, Sun Carrier, in order to receive the weapons and power to destroy the monsters which made life on earth so difficult. These stories are an important source of ceremonial validation. Chants and ritual performances have their source in this and other mythological accounts.

The singer, or medicine man, is called upon to perform ceremonies whose main function is curing. In order to determine what chant or ceremony is needed, a diviner (hand trembler or star gazer) is consulted. The medicine man is chosen on the basis of his skill in the ceremony to be performed. Out of a great number of ceremonies any given singer will be able to perform from one to a few. These ceremonies can last from one to five nights with larger public ceremonies lasting as long as nine nights. The ceremony usually begins with a dry painting made of sand and other dry materials depicting through symbolic figures, color, direction, etc., the mythological events on which the ceremony is based. The focus of the ceremony is the patient, but those who attend or participate believe that they absorb benefit from the power that is present in and around the ceremony.

Perhaps the word that best describes the Navajo spiritual outlook is "harmony." There is a delicate balance between man and the world around him. Taboo is set down in oral wisdom, mythology and experience. Violation of taboo upsets the harmony of things and a ceremony is required to "put things back again." It would be difficult for a person to live one day without breaking some taboo, but these infractions are not taken too seriously unless there is sickness, misfortune or tragedy. When this occurs, it's usually not too difficult to find a cause for it relating back to taboo.

It has been pointed out by many that Navajos have little or no interest in an after-life. It is true that there is not a lot of thought given to life after death, but there is definitely a belief that death does not end all. There may be a growing belief in another world due to the influence of Christianity.

Witchcraft

Witchcraft is both feared and used by the people. If trouble or tragedy cannot be explained by the breaking of taboo, etc., it can be blamed on witchcraft. If a ceremony does not bring about the desired results, it may be because of witchcraft. Also, if a person accumulates too many possessions and fails to share with relatives, he may be accused of witchcraft. A good discussion of the types of witchcraft practiced by the Navajo can be found in *Witchcraft Among the Navajo* by Clyde Kluckhohn.

Peyote

According to Marriott and Rachlin (1971:52), the Peyote cult was introduced to the Navajos in 1901 by a Comanche by the name of Red Fox who was thrown out of his tribe and took refuge among the Navajos. In 1971, the Native American Church (Peyote) claimed 40,000 members in Navajoland.

About 100 years ago, Quanah Parker, a half blood Comanche received peyote from a Mexican Indian woman who cared for him during a time of illness. He introduced it to his own people and from there it has rapidly spread through tribes in the United States and Canada. The Peyote cult, as it is often called, is a mixture of Christian and tribal elements. The all-night meetings are led by a Road Man (He Who Shows the Road) and the participants are seated around the crescent moon altar on which rests "Father Peyote," an especially fine specimen of a peyote button. The people chew the peyote or drink a tea made from ground peyote. This mild hallucinogen can produce visions in brilliant color if taken in sufficient quantity. Participants share their experiences with the group and these are interpreted in terms of their daily life and needs.

The Peyote movement was introduced by Indians, claims to belong to the Indians, and is a totally indigenous movement operating within the social framework of the Navajos. These facts no doubt contributed to the rapid growth of the Native American Church among the Navajos. The books on peyote listed in the bibliography are all in print and any one of them will give the reader an adequate knowledge of the Native American Church. Every Navajo missionary should be informed about a movement that claims 40,000+ members among the people.

NOTES

1. Children attending pre-school, kindergarten, and the Rough Rock Demonstration School receive instruction in Navajo.

BIBLIOGRAPHY

HODGE, WM. H.
    1969   The Albuquerque Navajos. University
           of Arizona Press, Tucson.

MARRIOTT, ALICE AND CAROL K. RACHLIN.
    1971   Peyote. New American Library, New York.

2
Navajo History Since 1541

PRE-SPANISH PERIOD

The Navajos were late comers to the Southwest.
They came to an area long inhabited by Pueblo Indians
and the Anasazi (derived from the Navajo word for an-
cient ones) or cliff dwellers like those who had
lived at Mesa Verde. It is believed from language similarities and
other evidences that ancestors of the Navajo lived to
the north in Canada and Alaska where Athabascan
speaking tribes still exist. They apparently mi-
grated south as a single ethnic group with a common
cultural core. They have now become nine Apache
tribes and one Navajo tribe. Linguists have calcu-
lated that the Navajo and Chiricahua Apache were
close relatives and historically very friendly. Their
languages became distinctive one from the other during a period of only 149 years. (Hoijer 1963, but
see Dutton 1975:9).
        The Navajo call themselves *dine'* (the people) or
T'áá Dine'e' (The People). In other words, the chosen
people. The name "Navajo" is not in the Navajo language and is of recent origin. The first written use
of the word occurs in 1626 when Fray Zarte Salmers
wrote of "Apaches de Nabaju" (Terrell 1972:37). The
name "Apache" comes from a Zuni word *A'pachu*, "enemy",
and it is believed "Navajo" is derived from the Tewa
word *Na'vaju'u*, the arroyo with the cultivated fields
(Dutton 1975:5). Enemies or strangers with the cultivated field was their descriptive designation.
        The Navajo first settled in *Dine'tah*, or old
Navajoland (literally "among the people"). Archaeol-
ogists have called the period dating from 1696 to

1775 the Gobernador phase (Dutton 1975:8). Gobernador
is located east of Farmington, New Mexico, and north
of Santa Fe where the Jicarilla Apache Reservation is
today. No one knows when the Navajos made their first
appearance into the Southwest, but some time prior to
1541. There are hoghan ruins near old Navajoland
scattered among the cliffs and junipers dating earlier than 1541 (Underhill 1956:18).
The Navajo-Apaches were a major contrast to the
old civilization of the Pueblos in the area. The
Pueblos lived in villages and the concern was for the
group as a whole, with little thought of the individual, allowing only for differences in minor traits.
In contrast, among the Navajo-Apaches, it is the
individual who is of primary importance (Dutton 1975:
3). As an individual-oriented society they had no
chief or priest as did their neighbors, but natural
leaders headed up small groups of related individuals. According to Dutton, they followed a patrilinial
system of descent with a patrilocal residence [1]. and
it is believed that they had a shaman-individualistic
religion preoccupied with curing (Dutton 1975:4). The
Apaches still retain this system today, but the Navajos have gone through notable periods of acculturation.

THE SPANISH CONTACT PERIOD
1582-1819

The Spanish contact came in 1582 when Antonio
de Espejo met "peaceful Indian mountaineers who
brought us tortillas even though we did not need
them." The mountaineers were Navajo (Terrell 1972:
22) living in the Mt. Taylor area. Don Juan de Oñate
brought the first Spanish colonists to settle in Northern New Mexico in 1598. Oñate raided the Pueblos
for grain and slaves and fought off counter raids
that nearly wiped out his colony. From the time of
Oñate, many of the Pueblos fled their homes to escape
Spanish oppression. Some went north and east, but
large numbers of them found a haven among the Navajos
who always welcomed refugees. Ruins of homes con-
structed of rock and adobe in traditional Pueblo
style have been found adjacent to the hoghans of the

Navajo settlements (Terrell 1972:28).
Terrell gives us a descriptive account of the
raids on the Keres, friends of the Navajos at Acoma.

> At the time the Keres and the Navajos
> were friends and traded with each other. If
> Navajos were not actually in the pueblo when
> the fight occurred, they were not far away
> for they were eyewitnesses to the terrible
> events that took place in January 1599,
> which insured their undying hostility toward
> the Spanish....
>
> Vincente gave no thought to leniency. In a
> few days he and his soldiers, none of whom
> was killed in the battle, murdered at least
> eight hundred men, women, and children. When
> the Keres begged for mercy and offered pay-
> ments of food and blankets, Vincente had
> prisoners brought out, cut to pieces, and
> their remains thrown off a cliff. Some five
> hundred women and children and eighty men
> were taken as captives to San Juan and there
> Oñate pronounced the punishment they were to
> receive. Males who were twenty-five years
> of age were to have a foot cut off and were
> to labor in "personal servitude" for twenty
> years. Younger males and all women were
> sentenced to slavery. Girls under the age
> of twelve were given to Fray Alonso Martinez
> who was to distribute them as he wished to
> Spanish families "in this kingdom or else-
> where" (Terrell 1972:30,31).

By 1630, the Navajos numbered in the thousands.
They were less vulnerable to Spanish attacks, living
as they did in scattered camps and being mobile. The
Spanish might kill some of them, but never all of
them. By this time they were scattered far from
Dinetah and were distinguished by their mobility and
wide distribution. Trading as part of their economy
was second in importance only to raiding. The
Spaniards and Navajos warred against each other for
140 years and atrocities were committed by both

sides. To the Navajo, it was a way of life and they
made themselves a difficult target.   The Pueblos, on
the other hand, were easy marks for a surrounding
army of Spaniards with horses and guns.   Many Pueblo
villages were completely destroyed and their inhabitants fled to the Navajos. Pueblos and Navajos became √
partners with a common enemy.   The Spaniards raided
for stolen livestock and for grain, but the most
sought-after prize was slaves.   Men were usually
killed, but women and children were taken alive, baptized, used for servants and sold as slaves.   An average Navajo boy or girl aged five to fifteen brought
as high as $200 on the auction block   (Terrell 1972:
116).
     Navajos raided for sheep, horses, material ob-
jects and slaves. The philosophy of the Navajos was
defined in their maxim: "Poor is the man who can see
farther than his horses graze."   Their acquisitive-
ness extended to all domestic animals, but horses
were prized above all.   Horses were riches, and in
the reasoning of the Navajos there could be no such
thing as a surplus.   Today unprofitable horses con-
sume the sparse grass, limiting the feed for the profitable sheep and cattle.   But still the sight of
horses grazing as far as one can see is a sight of
beauty to the Navajo owner.
     Despite the disasters they suffered one after
another at the hands of the Spaniards, the Navajo and √
Pueblos continued to make plans for a united revolt.
"Death and devastation appeared to act as fertilizer
for the seeds of rebellion" (Terrell 1972:52).   In
August of 1680 the bomb exploded.   √

     Navajos and Pueblos, under the generalship of
     Popé, a medicine man of San Juan, swept
     through northern New Mexico in waves too pow-
     erful to be resisted.   It was a well-planned
     and well-executed uprising. Quickly more than
     four hundred colonists and twenty-one priests
     were slain.   A few of the most attractive
     women were taken alive and turned over to the
     Indian leaders for their pleasure. The Span-
     iards, converted Indians, and servants who
     escaped the initial onsloughts fled to Santa

Fe and barricaded themselves with Governor
Otermin and other residents of the capital in
government buildings. There, for ten days,
they successfully withstood assaults by several thousand warriors.

The province of New Mexico was abandoned to
the Indians. Determined to destroy every
trace of the invaders, they continued to ram-
page through the land, burning the Spanish
churches and missions, their factories, farms
and homes. And every person who had been for-
cibly baptized by the Franciscans was
scrubbed with yucca suds (Terrell 1972:54).

THE PUEBLO ACCULTURATION PERIOD
1819-1846

During the twelve-year period when the Spaniards
were gone, the Navajos welcomed their Pueblo com-
patriots in large numbers. In the space of a few
years the Navajo adopted the Puebloan manufacturing
techniques and religious paraphernalia, adapting it
to their mobile existence. A Navajo medicine man
would carry all the paraphernalia needed in a "jish"
(bag) and hold ceremonies from place to place at the
request of the people. In Pueblo life such mobility
was unnecessary and the paraphernalia remained large
and cumbersome. Many elements of non-material culture such as clans, matrilinial descent, matrilocal
residence, the origin myth and ritual became incorporated into Navajo religion (Dutton 1975:8). Other
Pueblo influence included sand paintings, metate and
fire pit styles and, in part, weaving. All of these
altered the basic Navajo culture and distinguished it
from that of the Apaches who were less in contact
with the Pueblo peoples. Although the Navajos adopted Pueblo agriculture, manufacturing techniques and
ceremonials, they did not become Pueblos. The reason
is that they absorbed those customs they believed
would benefit them and those that most delighted and
appealed to them, but rejected all other Pueblo ways
of life. They became competent farmers, but they did
not give up raiding. They accepted the Pueblo "religious riches," but not without adapting them to their
own thinking. They used the Pueblo "framework of

theology and ceremony, but into it they poured their
own feeling for movement and some of the lore of
every region they had traversed" (Terrell 1972:59)
and healing or curing remained the central rite.
Mexican control covered the period of 1821-1846.
The Navajo saw no difference between them and the
Spaniards.

                     THE AMERICAN CONTACT PERIOD
                            1846-1950
The American contact period began in 1846 with
the arrival of General S.W.Kearny and the U. S. Army.
Treaties again were signed and broken. The Americans,
as their Spanish and Mexican predecessors, failed to
take into account the Navajo decision-making process;
no Navajo makes decisions for other Navajos. Someone
may act as spokesman for his relatives and those in
his immediate area with their consent and he is their
naat'áanii, their talker (literally the one whose
head moves from side to side as he speaks). Other
camps have their own *naat'áanii*, who may represent
them to a limited degree, but ultimately everything
is up to the individual. Certainly, no Navajo could
presume to speak for all Navajos and signing of treaties were only binding on those who signed and on no
others. Broken treaties were incomprehensible to
Americans, but pretending to speak for others without
their consent was incomprehensible to Navajos.
     From 1846-1863 there were continuous Navajo "up-
risings." Forts and garrisons to control the upris-
ings were generally left unmanned following the out-
break of the civil war of 1861. The Navajo and
Apaches were quick to take advantage of the situation
and some were the scourge of the countryside. Colonel
Christopher (Kit) Carson from Taos was called to lead
a campaign against the Navajo. This was a policy of
General James Carleton and was carried out to re-
settle the Navajo and Apaches at Ft. Sumner, New
Mexico. They were to become farmers like the Pueblos.
All captives who surrendered voluntarily would be
taken there and all male Navajos who resisted would
be shot. Their livestock and food supplies were to
be destroyed, and they were (Dutton 1975:11).
     By December 1865, the Navajos at Ft. Sumner num-
bered 8,354. In the next year 1,200 escaped and

returned to Navajoland. No one knows how many Navajo
escaped captivity entirely. At Red Mesa, Arizona,
Grace Oldman tells how her great grandfather was too
old to make the trip to Ft. Sumner. He was left behind by the army in a hoghan to die, but a son and
his wife were left behind by the Navajos to take care
of the old man. They hid in the rocks on Dry Mesa
going down around midnight every night to see about
the old man. If no soldiers were staying in the
hoghan to catch them, the old man, nearly blind,
would tap with his cane on the dirt floor of the
hoghan and his son would come in bringing water and
food from their supplies (interview with Grace
Oldman, 1969). In this way part of the family escaped
capture and removal to Ft. Sumner.

Unforgettable, second only to the "long walk" in
Navajo-American relations, is the stock reduction
program. The Navajo agent Collier, who had painstakingly built a good relationship with the Navajo,
pushed through a stock reduction program before the
people were educated to accept it. Again, Grace
Oldman tells what happened to her family. In the
first reduction in 1934, her father, Hostiin
Kitseally, a man with 2,000 head of livestock and
sheep, was forced to reduce them to 400. Then, in
1937, he was again asked to comply with the order to
reduce his herds, this time to 80. He refused to
comply. He was arrested, taken to Prescott and jailed
for thirty days. His family was not at home at the
time and did not know what had become of him. His
wife was pregnant when his livestock were forcefully
taken and destroyed. Navajos were paid $2 to $5 per
head for the sheep and forced to drive them off a
cliff. At Red Mesa the young people point out that
cliff and describe the wanton destruction of "their"
sheep. Such a memory is etched in the minds of the
Navajo and the resulting hatred of the white man is
passed on to each generation. (Interview and personal
conversations 1969).

These two events, more than anything else, made
the Navajo people a non-receptive people to American
missionaries during their first fifty years of missionary activity. Undoubtedly, if missionaries had
come from a culture other than the Spanish (Catholic)

and American (Protestant) cultures, the Navajo would
have been responsive. All other factors indicate
Navajos readily accepted new ideas, especially if
they were coming from those they considered to be
their friends.

The Navajo readily borrow from other cultures ?
giving each cultural item or idea their own twist.
From the Spanish contact period came material acquisitions including their colorful dress that the older
women still wear today, their sheep and more. They
ate the sheep from their first raids, but more and
more raiders accumulated herds and became wealthy.
The wealthy then vied for peace with the Spaniards
but the poor continued to raid, seeing how it had ma-
terially benefited their neighbors. Horses were the
most highly prized acquisition from the Spaniards because they gave one the ability to raid effectively
and to be even more mobile. Several money terms in
Navajo are of Spanish derivative *(béeso, głinsii,
yáál)*. In all, about fifteen words are of Spanish
derivative.

These material borrowings greatly affected
Navajo life and culture, but Navajos remained imper- ✓
vious to Catholic religion. At times, they let "the
fathers throw water on them", (Spicer, p.299), but
only when it was to their material gain; when it no
longer served their purposes they readily walked away
from it.

On the other hand, during this time Navajo religion became overlayed with Pueblo religion, especially
that of the Hopi. The greatest acculturation came in
the 1680's and 90's. We might picture this overlay
like this:

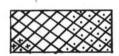

Navajo-Apache   Pueblo Overlay
Cultural Core   + Christian
                           · Peyote

Terrell says, "the Navajos are materialists" and
are readily willing to make material acquisitions
from anyone if they can see how it will benefit them,

but only adopt religious change from their friends. After witnessing the first Spanish massacre of the Keres, the Spanish became their arch enemies. Hopes of converting them to Catholocism in a meaningful way was doomed from that time. There was much contact with the Pueblos during the period of 1682-1696 when the latter's villages were destroyed and the Navajos and Pueblos became allies against the Spanish. Navajos readily accepted religious concepts and patterns from the Pueblos forming a whole new cohesive religion that has come down to the present and is called *dine´k'ehjígo*, "the Navajo way."

THE AMERICAN ACCULTURATION PERIOD
1950-1978

Housing Changes

As recent as twelve years ago, tourists could travel the new highway across the northern part of the Reservation and never see the homes of the Navajo. They built them away from the highway and the hoghans blended perfectly with the landscape. Today nearly every camp has one or more frame houses in addition to the hoghan. Along the highway, electricity is usually available and in some rural communities a water system brings inside water and modern plumbing to the Navajo. Between Denehotso and Kayenta, a 20 mile stretch, 21 camps are visible containing 27 frame and mud hoghans, 30 houses and 7 trailer houses. Over half of these camps have electricity and 15 T.V. antennas protrude from hoghans, houses and trailers. Navajo young people are "hooked" on T.V., as are most of the adults who understand English. Its acculturating effect in the next few years is incalculable.

Urbanized communities like Shiprock and Tuba City are experiencing a tremendous growth of people of all ages, especially young couples attracted by electricity, television, jobs and modern housing. A dramatic change in sense of community and belonging arises from living next to non-relatives and total strangers.

The forked-stick hoghan described by earlier writers as essential to sings and ceremonies is seen almost nowhere. The female or "secular" hoghan is

now used for sings and occasionally frame hoghans
with cement floors are used as well.

Funeral and Marriage Changes

Only rarely is a funeral conducted in the traditional way. The handling of the dead corpse was
readily given over to the missionary and more recently, in urbanized areas, to the mortician. Funerals
follow western cultural patterns entirely,or in part.
In rural areas the 4th night meeting still occurs.
People are buried, for the most part, in mission or
public cemeteries.

Marriages are occasionally held in the traditional way where the parents arrange the wedding, but
more and more the young people "fall in love" at
school or work and the wedding is a western, traditional ceremony at the church, chapter house, or in a
home. Sometimes the two traditions are blended.

Girls' clothing is dominated by Levi pants and
blouses, common among many American young people.
Halters and backless blouses and shorts are appearing
in increasing numbers since catching your own man now
requires more feminine ingenuity, to say nothing of
peer pressure to dress in the new style.

Transportation

Ten to fifteen years ago, only a limited number
of Navajo families had cars and pickups. At Red Mesa,
only three or four pickups existed. Today, new pickups, paved roads and cars are making a mobile people
able to go whenever and wherever they want to go. The
people are no longer tied to the trading, credit and
pawn system at the trading post. There is more cash
flow and less dependence on the trader. The rural
sheep herding - livestock culture is being rapidly
transformed into a job oriented culture operating on
a new time piece, the clock instead of the sun.

Cross-Cultural Conflicts

All of this acculturation brings tension, a tension from the desire to acquire more of the material-
ism of western culture and a fear of losing the *diné
k'ehjígo*, the Navajo way, as other Indian tribes have
lost theirs.

There is a generation gap between the unschooled older generation and the younger generation. When young people return from boarding school, traditionally the older family members hold a ceremony for them. They say, "They have become disobedient, disrespectful children and need to be purified ceremonially from the constant contact with Anglos." The young people reluctantly comply. When Anglo visitors come to the Navajo house or hoghan, the young people are embarrassed and hide because of the contrast in their modest home and the Anglos' luxurious housing and material acquisitions. All of this leads to a strong dissatisfaction with the status quo and the desire to have what the white people have.

Young people have to behave in one way at home and adjust to an entirely different pattern of behavior and set of expectations at school. School teachers, unfamiliar with the culture, appear abrasive, rude and bossy to Navajo young people. They are given such nicknames as *Tl'izi Cho'* (billie goat) because they push people around like a billie goat. All Navajo young people know the significance of these nicknames but the teacher never does. To the teachers, the children are backward, uncooperative and stubborn because they will not volunteer information. In Navajo culture, it is wrong for a child to show off his knowledge. In his culture, it is not proper to be competitive. It is proper to be non-competitive.

Communication, both spoken and unspoken, signals different meanings and reactions in the two cultures. The classic comparison is the difference in communication in dog-and-cat cultures. To dogs, the wagging of the tail communicates friendliness. To the cat, the raising of the tail means hostility. Extending the paw to the dog means, "I want to play." To the cat it means, "He is trying to claw me. He wants to fight." To the cat raising his back while he is purring means "pet me." To the dog raising his back while growling means "I am going to attack you."

To the Anglo teacher, the child who won't look her in the eye is trying to hide something. The teacher will often demand that the child look at her while the teacher is speaking. To the Navajo child, looking one in the eyes is taboo and very impolite.

When an Anglo drives into the yard of a Navajo family
and sees everyone go into the house and close the
door, it means to the Anglo, "We don't want to talk
to you" but, to the Navajo it means, "We are stopping
our work just for you and are awaiting your visit."
    Such misunderstanding of non-verbal communica-
tion cross-culturally results in cultural conflicts.
Undoubtedly, failure of communication is the greatest
cause of Anglo-Navajo tension.
    Cross-cultural tensions that occur when a minor-
ity group comes into inevitable contact with the dominant society have played their part in making the
Navajos a resistive field. In fact, Navajos remained ✓
impervious to the Gospel for many years. Navajos were
not, however, resistant to religious change. During
the past 40 years, many were swept into the Peyote
cult which was introduced on the Reservation in 1938.
The rapid growth of the Native Church of North
America, as they call themselves, indicates that a
religious void existed and that the Navajos were
looking for religious fulfillment and change. During
this time about 8% of the people have become church
attenders while perhaps 40% have turned to Peyote.The
latter was advocated by Indians from other tribes,the
former was advocated by white men. Peyote was rapidly introduced within the Navajo social structure and
Christianity remained a foreign entity until recently. Peyote was advocated by other Indians and then
Navajo innovaters became the advocates. Christianity ✓
was advocated by Anglos and in their typical ethno-
centricism they were reluctant to trust the Navajo
and the Holy Spirit dwelling within them with the
Scriptures and the Church. Fear of "heresies," some
founded and some unfounded, created an Anglo captivity of the Navajo churches which they are only now beginning to overcome.

NOTES

[1.]An interesting hypothesis yet to be proven.

BIBLIOGRAPHY

DUTTON, BERTHA P.
   1975   Navajo and Apaches: the Athabascan
          Peoples. Prentice Hall Inc. Englewood
          Cliffs, N.J.

TERRELL, JOHN UPTON
   1972   The Navajos. Harper and Row, New York,
          N.Y.

UNDERHILL, RUTH
   1956   The Navajo. University of Oklahoma Press,
          Norman, Oklahoma.

Part Two

Coming to Jesus

3
Navajo Churches and Missions: A Brief History

No over all history of missions on the Navajo Reservation has been written. Some histories of single denominations or missions have been or are being written. This brief sketch is from the present written material available to us and from those responses to the questionnaire that was sent out to the missions.

THE INITIAL CONTACT PERIOD
1869-1912

The Catholic contact period began with Spanish conquests of the Southwest. As early as 1774 attempts were made to establish missions among the Navajo (Spicer, Ed., 1961, p.298). These initial contacts were very superficial and no permanent work existed until the beginning of St. Michael's Mission in 1901.

Protestant contact was made first by the Presbyterians in 1869. The Treaty of 1868 allowed the Navajo to return to the bounds of the Reservation it defined. It also committed the United States government to certain obligations for schooling the Navajo children. In order to find teachers the government turned to the churches.

Fort Defiance

Responding to this need for teachers was a Presbyterian minister, Rev. James M. Roberts. The Roberts arrived in Fort Defiance in 1869 and began school in the fall with an average attendance of 14. Miss Charity Gaston was sent as a paid government teacher

soon after. She was to teach in the school begun by
Roberts under a government "peace policy" whose announced aim was to "civilize and Christianize the
Navajo."   In vivid language Terrell describes this
first school.

> A leaky mudwalled hovel that was to be
> both classroom and home....
> The rough log benches of the school
> could have accommodated twenty-five pupils,
> but there were never that many present,even
> during the most pleasant weather. Some
> mornings three or four would arrive, cling-
> ing to one another on a pony. On other days
> six or seven might appear. On many days the
> classroom remained empty.   Rarely did the
> same children attend on two consecutive
> days, or even on any two days in one month.
> Occasionally, two or three Navajo women
> would come to spend an hour staring incred-
> ulously at the young woman with pompadour
> and combs, immaculate in her neat white
> shirtwaist, long woolen skirt, and high
> shoes. They would giggle and chatter unin-
> telligibly, but with obvious appreciation
> if she served them lunch.
> A number of the children were notice-
> ably retarded or unwell. The agent said
> that some families sent sickly boys and
> girls to the school in the hope that they
> would be cured of their afflictions. If
> they were killed by exposure to "book
> magic" the loss would not be great(Terrell,
> 246-247).

Charity Gaston married the doctor at the post in
1872 and she and Dr. Menaul then moved to a pueblo of
the Laguna.   The Presbyterians continued to supply
teachers.   J. D. Perkins came in 1880 and buildings
were enlarged.   They were made of hugh thick rock
walls to accommodate 150 to 200 students, but not
nearly this many could be enrolled.   In 1897,Congress
changed the law making it the policy that "The Government hereafter to make no appropriation whatever

to   subsidize   sectarian   schools   serving   Indian
groups."
     Mission work was Mr. Roberts' department and the
mission only lasted three years.   Roberts was especially frustrated   by   the   language   barrier and the
difficulty of learning Navajo, but he astutely evalu-
ated cultural foreignness   of books   and schooling to
the Navajo. He wrote:

> Now as to the system to be pursued in
> teaching of these Indians, I have already
> tried depending on the children coming to
> recite until I am satisfied that a school
> will not flourish and a desire among the
> people to educate will never be developed.
> They must be made to appreciate the advan-
> tages accruing from education. The very
> fact of the children becoming tired of re-
> citing every day, what seems to both old
> and young mere nonsense, which is almost
> always the case as soon as the novelty is
> worn off, will only tend to prejudice the
> parents against the education of the chil-
> dren and the result will be hatred on the
> part of all for anything in the shape of a
> book... My idea is, of course, to get the
> language as soon as I can so as to communi-
> cate with them and thus exert an influence
> for good in that way but to raise up at the
> same time native teachers and set the tribe
> on an independent footing...A Navajo having
> learned English and being able to preach
> the Gospel will have a weight of influence
> among them which an American preacher could
> not wield in any way (Smith and Nelson,8).

     After three years, the birth of a son and the
illness of his wife, a discouraged Roberts moved to
Taos, New Mexico, and the first Protestant mission
effort came to an end. One can only wish that a man
of his perception had remained to see his vision
begin to materialize.
     Fort Defiance proved to be a discouraging place
to plant a church for some time. The Methodists tried
in 1888 and abandoned it.   The   Christian   Reformed

missionaries,   Mr. and Mrs. Andrew Vanderwagen and
Rev. and Mrs. Herman Fryling arrived in Fort Defiance
in October of 1896. After one year, the Vanderwagens
left to begin work in Zuni, New Mexico. The Frylings
stayed until 1906, during which time Rev. Fryling initiated   a program of religious instruction in the
government school that became a major part of all
missionary endeavor until recent years.
     The Episcopalians arrived in Fort Defiance in
1897 and started a medical work that resulted in Good
Shepherd hospital and church. This work was pioneered
by a nurse, Miss Thagara. The Presbyterians arrived
sometime before 1912, because the report shows that
in 1912, the Presbyterian Church had one organized
church among the Navajo and that was at Fort Defiance
(Smith and Nelson, 68).

Jewett and Farmington

     In the year 1891, two pioneer Methodist mission-
ary women arrived in Jewett Valley, west of Farmington.   They were Mary Louise Eldredge and Mary E.
Raymond. They had had previous cross cultural experience with Indians at Haskell Indian School   in
Lawrence, Kansas, and on the Pine River Reservation
in South Dakota. They lived in a tent until an adobe
house could be built. They became involved in irri-
gation and other programs of social betterment. Mary
Eldredge divided her time between her mission and a
government job among the Navajo.
     They started a Sunday school for the Anglo chil-
dren and a few of their parents who lived in the Jewett area. Also during this time they made trips on
horseback into the Chuska Mountains on the Reservation. On one such trip they report finding gardens
ready to harvest but saw no Navajo people. One won-
ders if the elusive Navajo made themselves unavail-
able to the white women intruders.
     They were later joined by Frank Damon,who became
the interpreter, and by Mary Tripp, a school teacher.
Thomas Harwood organized a church training class for
Navajos on May 1, 1898. In 1896, Mary Tripp opened a
day school with only Anglo students, and in 1899 she
started a boarding school with 13 Navajo boarding
students and 20 Anglo day students (Malehorn, 1-30).

This was the first continuously operating Navajo mission school on the Reservation. The property at Jewett was sold to the Presbyterians in 1903 for $1000 and was moved to the junction of the LaPlata and San Juan Rivers where it was flooded and destroyed in 1911. The school was rebuilt in 1912 at its present site in Framington, New Mexico, and is called Navajo Methodist Mission School (McDonald and Arrington, 92).

The Methodists started no other churches for 40 years after the little one at Jewett. Rather, they considered their mission to the Navajo to be in the field of education.

Tuba City and Navajo Mountain

John Butler came to Tuba City in 1894 under the auspices of The Gospel Union Mission. In 1896 he was joined by Ethel Sawyer and Jennie June Johnson, also with the Gospel Union Mission. These two women at one time traveled on a burro making initial contacts with the Navajo people and presenting the claims of Jesus as far away as Navajo Mountain.

While at Navajo Mountain, a medicine man hired a boy to kill the women's burro; without transportation their shoes wore out. They were taken in by a Navajo family during a snowstorm and stayed until they could travel. The Navajo man made them each a pair of moccasins and when the weather permitted they walked out. Their unplanned stay with this family proved fruitful. Many years later (1964) Bruce Yazzie, a well known Navajo preacher in the western part of the Reservation, visited a remote hoghan at Navajo Mountain and was surprised to hear them praying to the One Living God and to hear this family say that they had heard the Gospel many years before. They told Bruce of the two women who spent part of the winter in their hoghan. One old woman testified she had been a believer since she first heard the Gospel (conversation with Dr. David Clark, son of Ethel Sawyer Clark).

Ethel Sawyer married Dr. Sipe in Flagstaff and their home became a stopping place for early Presbyterian missionaries going to the Reservation. Dr. and Mrs. Sipe initiated the medical work for the Christian Reformed at Rehoboth and Dr. Sipe died soon

after.   Mrs. Ethel Sipe later married   Howard Clark,
who had come to their home   in Flagstaff as a young
Presbyterian seminary graduate in 1907.

Tolchaco
     Mr. W. R. Johnston   also joined Mr. Butler at
Tuba City in 1896 under the Gospel Union Mission. Mr.
Johnston moved to Tolchaco near Leupp, Arizona, and
formed an "independent" mission with the help of Mr.
Butler.   Fred Mitchell and his 70 year old mother
joined Mr. Johnston in 1904.   These men started a
training school for Navajos to learn to preach the
Gospel in their own language and cultural context.
One of their students, J. C. Morgan, came all the way
from Shiprock, New Mexico. J. C. Morgan was a force-
ful preacher at Shiprock and in that area of the Reservation,   and in 1938 he became the Navajo Tribal
Chairman.
     The Johnstons moved to Indian Wells in 1906 and
began a new work with a medical service. Mrs.
Johnston was a nurse and nursed Navajos in her home.
Later a hospital was built.
     The Navajo preacher training school at Tolchaco
came under the auspices of the Presbyterians in 1914
and was destroyed by fire in 1918.   Fred Mitchell
tried to start the school again in Fort Defiance, but
was persuaded by the Presbyterians to become superintendent of Ganado Mission in 1921.   He lamented that
if "I had stayed in the training school at Tolchaco I
could have trained enough Navajo men to evangelize
the entire Reservation" (Salsbury, 1941:25).
     Johnston and Mitchell translated early portions
of Scripture. In about 1913 Fred Mitchell was driving
a team with a load of lumber to Tolchaco when the
team ran away. He fell under the wagon and it rolled
over him, breaking his back.   While convalescing in
bed in Tolchaco the Lord used him to write the Navajo
Language book, *Dineh Bizaad, a Handbook for Beginners
in the Study of the Navajo Language*. It was published
by the Board of National Missions of the Presbyterian
Church, USA.
     Fred Mitchell spent his early life on the Reser-
vation "sleeping in hoghans and sharing the food of
the people.....He was the first Protestant missionary

to use the Navajo language fluently and his ability
to talk in their own language strengthened his hold
on his chosen people" (Means, 1955:37).

Ganado

From 1872 - 1901 (following the departure of
Roberts from Fort Defiance) the Presbyterian Church
did not have an established mission on the Reservation, although Presbyterian individuals were involved
in the Tuba City and Tolchaco Gospel Union Mission
efforts. [1].

The Presbyterian Church at Flagstaff where Ethel
Sawyer (now the wife of Dr. Sipe) lived and worked
was moved to start the first permanent Presbyterian
Mission. Thomas Moffatt, a former pastor, and Dr.
George Logie, the current pastor, had developed a
special interest in and concern for the Navajo. Per-
suading the Presbytery of Arizona, they embarked on a
journey from Flagstaff to the east with the express
purpose of locating a site for a Presbyterian mission
in Arizona.

They started on this journey in April 1901, with
the women and children in a wagon with Mr. W. R.
Johnston. The women and children were left at
Tolchaco with the Johnston family and the men continued on horseback. Across the Hopi Mesas following an
old wagon trail they came to Oraibi where Dr. Logie's
eye was treated by the Reformed Church missionary.
Later they were given a warm welcome at Keams Canyon
by Mr. Thayer, a Baptist missionary. Later it was on
to Ganado where Lorenzo Hubbell, a trader since 1868
and a good Catholic, welcomed them and graciously
hosted them. With Mr. Hubbell's help the men select-
ed a mission site (Smith and Nelson, 36,37).

Within a year, Rev. Charles H. Bierkemper was
sent to Ganado as the missionary. He left after a
few months to marry his fianceé and returning they
moved into an adobe house provided by Mr. Hubbell. In
the dining room of their home, Mrs. Bierkemper started a Navajo Day School. Mr. Bierkemper was a mason
by trade and after building a house on the hundred
acre mission site, he built a church building in 1906
(Smith and Nelson, 38).

Converts were won painstakingly. It was not

until 1913 that a church was organized with seven
members. These members included Denasbah (Martha
Conklin), Dasbah Curley and Guy Kedohahii Clark
(Salsbury: 1941, 23).
Mr. Bierkemper describes the first conversion:

> Grandmother Lois was one of the first
> Navajo women to make regular visits to the
> Mission. After she came to church, she was
> called "Woman Preacher." Once we went out
> to visit her and found her herding sheep.We
> sat on the ground and preached to her and
> she decided to accept Christ. Later, her
> folks threatened to poison her, so she de-
> cided to wait a little while before she
> joined the church. Then she became ill. I
> went to see her and found her surrounded by
> medicine men. I was told that she had lis-
> tened so much to the White people that the
> devil had gotten into her. After an argu-
> ment, I was able to take her to the Mis-
> sion; she stayed in bed a few days and then
> she was able to go back to sheep herding.
> Shortly after that she joined the Church as
> our first convert. She had no more trouble
> with the Medicine Men, but was a shining
> light for the Master (Smith and Nelson,39).

Keams Canyon

When Dr. Logie and the group of Presbyterians
came through Keams Canyon, he notes that they were
welcomed by a Baptist missionary, Mr. Thayer. So we
know that Mr. Thayer was at Keams Canyon in 1901.
Mr. Thayer erected the first church building at
Keams Canyon in 1913. At the close of the dedication
service, ten charter members established the first
church organization. Before Mr. Thayer left in 1923,
most of the adult members had moved away. Work with
the school children and in the homes continued under
the leadership of other workers, but a formal church
organization could not be maintained. Each year a
preparation class was held for young converts from
the school. From twenty to forty were baptized at
the end of the year, but there was no longer an organized church in which their membership could be

placed (Bucklin, 58-59).

Tohatchi

The Christian Reformed missionary Andrew Vander-
Wagen visited Tohatchi irregularly in 1898 and a permanent resident worker, James E. DeGroot, came in
1899. However, Mr. DeGroot had to leave because of
the altitude.

Rev. L. P. Brink came in 1900 and began a long ✓
and illustrious missionary career. A church building
was built in 1910 and is still used today after several remodelings. During the thirteen years that
L. P. Brink was at Tohatchi, he learned the Navajo
language and, with the help of the Navajo people,
translated hymns. The hymns were published and
taught to the people and they were taught to read in
their own Navajo language. Many people came to church
at this time (DeKorne, 61-66).

Rehoboth

Land was secured for a mission site at Rehoboth
in 1903 by Miss Nellie Noordhof and a small school
was started. A chapel was erected and children and
staff attended but adult Navajos could not be induced
to attend. At Rehoboth a different philosophy of
missions came into play. It was the philosophy underlying Ganado and the Methodist Mission at Farmington.
The philosophy was one of "educate, civilize, and in-
dustrialize" in order to evangelize the Navajo.

Therefore, the missionaries were instructed to
look for a suitable location for an industrial insti-
tution where we would be able to colonize our future
converts and provide wages and means for them to
enjoy a Christian life (Beets, 46). Establishment of
a bakery, trading post, textile enterprise and a
school was the goal of this location. There can be ✓✓
no argument against these attempts to improve condi-
tions economically, educationally and medically, but
subsequent years have shown them ineffective as a
means of evangelism. Where establishing churches and
preaching the Gospel has been the sole goal,
evangelism of the Navajo has been more effective.

This was the philosophy of other pioneer missionaries who held that "uplift of the Indians was to

be principally by the propagation of the Gospel"
(Southwest Bible and Missionary Conference 70th Anni-
versary Publication, no author, no date, no publisher). That difference in philosophy has persisted in
mission work around the world.

Rehoboth Conference in 1907
An important conference held in Rehoboth in
these early years is described in *Southwest Bible and
Missionary Conference 70th Anniversary Publication* (no
author, no date, no publisher). This was a conference
of an interdenominational organization of Hopi, Zuni
and Navajo missionaries called "Friends of the
Indians." This organization was formed in 1903. W.R.
Johnston from Tuba City was chosen as chairman and J.
Epp from Oraibi was secretary. This group met in
Flagstaff in 1904 and 1905 and at Ganado in 1906. By
1907 there were forty members representing Presbyterian, Baptist, Christian Reformed, Mennonite and
Gospel Union missionaries. The forty members also
included one Pima, two Navajos and three Hopis.
The meeting at Rehoboth was described in some
detail:

> Considerable hardship attended the un-
> daunted scores who came to the Rehoboth
> conference on horseback and in covered wag-
> ons. Several schooner wagons joined together
> at Oraibi. More and more joined the proces-
> sion as the caravan joyfully and expectantly
> journeyed on toward Rehoboth, and drenching
> rains failed to cool the enthusiasm of these
> and half a hundred other travelers*(Southwest
> Conference 70th Anniversary Publication,* no
> author, no date, no publisher).

Discussions revolved around these topics:

What are we here for?   F. C. Ried, Pastor
              Presbyterian Church, Flagstaff, AZ.

Value of, and methods in itinerating
                              John Butler
              Gospel Union Mission, Tuba City, AZ.

The missionary's relation to the
  industrial and material advance-
  ment of the Indian   Herman Fryling
                     Christian Reformed, Rehoboth, AZ.

How much of the native language
  should the missionary know?   J. B. Frey

Our fields and their needs   L. P. Brink
                     Christian Reformed, Tohatchi, N.M.

Prayer and the sanctified life   Fred Mitchell
                     Gospel Union Mission, Tolchaco, AZ.

       "It was agreed that the uplift of the Indians
was to be principally by the propagation of the Gospel" *(Southwest Conference 70th Anniversary Publication*, no author, no date, no publisher).
       A tentative agreement on the division of the
Navajo field for the respective denominations was
made, but that division was not stated. It resulted,
however, in the Presbyterians becoming responsible
for Arizona and the Christian Reformed for New
Mexico. The Baptists confined their work to Keams
Canyon and the work of the Gospel Union Mission continued a few years and then ceased to exist. The
Mennonites worked among the Hopi.
       The committee on Unification of Language Work
(L. P. Brink, Fred Mitchell and John Butler) reported
on their progress. The conference recommended one or
two years of language study for all workers, the
"means to be provided by respective boards." *(South
west Conference 70th Anniversary Publication*, no author, no date, no publisher). This conference met
annually and still exists today as the Southwest
Bible and Missionary Conference and meets at their
own campground in Flagstaff annually.

EARLY YEARS OF CHURCH PLANTING
1912-1949

During this period of time, the Christian Reformed Church started twelve churches:

1912	Crownpoint
1916	Toadlena
1922	Fort Wingate
1923	Canyoncito (discontinued)
1924	Farmington
1926	Naschitti
1928	San Antone
1930	Two Wells
1932	Sanostee
1932	Gallup Bethany
1934	Shiprock (took over Presbyterian work)
1934	Teec Nos Pos (took over Presbyterian work)
1930	Star Lake (discontinued)

Five of these churches were started by L. P. Brink and the others were begun by A. VanderWagen, H. Fryling, W. Mierop, G. Oppenhuizen, J. Bolt, J. W. Brink, J. Kobes, C. Hayenga, L. Henry, J. Tsosie and J. C. Morgan.

Many other preaching points were maintained by these missionaries. A large number of Christian Reformed men and women came to staff these mission churches and the mission compound at Rehoboth. A list of them and Navajo lay workers can be found in *The Navajo and Zuni for Christ* by J. C. DeKorne.

In 1946, the Christian Reformed Churches on the Reservation had 859 members, but not nearly this many were active. "The fact that so many of our converts came into our church in Navajoland too young, unripe, not fully comprehending what they were doing, explains the great difference between our roll of nominal members and that of our active members" (DeKorne, 114).

The Presbyterians started churches at Shiprock and Teec Nos Pos about the turn of the century; then during the depression they sold their buildings to the Christian Reformed Church.

In Arizona, the Presbyterians organized the

following churches after 10 to 26 years of pioneer
missionary work at each location:

	Work Begun	Church Organized
Fort Defiance	1869	1912
Ganado	1901	1915
Tuba City	1894*	1916
Chinle	1907	1921
Indian Wells	1906*	1923
Tolchaco	1896*	1914
Leupp	?	1924
Kayenta	1913	1939

*indicates those begun by Gospel Union Mission

Such a long period of plowing the ground and
planting the seed before seeing the harvest was not
unusual during this period of time.

In 1919, the Navajo population was estimated to
be 20,000 people. The Presbyterian Church had eight
stations and preaching points. Membership in the four
organized churches was: (Smith and Nelson, 68)

```
Tolchaco-Leupp....................51
Fort Defiance.....................46
Tuba City.........................46
Ganado............................16
```

In 1944, there were 640 members in the seven
Presbyterian churches, predominantly young people.
Pioneer missionaries and early church planters were
Fred Mitchell, Charles Bierkemper, Anthony Locker,
Hugh D. Smith, and Charles Bysegger (Smith and Nelson
69).

The Baptists worked among the Navajos at Keams
Canyon and trained the Stokelys who started Navajo
Gospel Mission at Hardrock in 1932, but the Baptists
themselves never expanded or planted other churches.

The Gospel Union Mission after their years of
pioneering at Tuba City, Tolchaco, Indian Wells,
Navajo Mountain and producing stalwarts like W. R.
Johnston, John Butler, Ethel Sawyer and Fred Mitchell
were absorbed by the Presbyterians.

The Episcopalians, in addition to the Good Shepherd Mission in Fort Defiance, started a church. In 1917 they started a mission and church in Farmington, New Mexico, a church at Fruitland, New Mexico, a church at Carson, New Mexico, and a preaching point at Shiprock, New Mexico. In 1943 they began at Bluff and Montezuma Creek, Utah.

The Plymouth Brethren started Immanuel Mission at Sweetwater, Arizona, in 1922. The Stokelys started Navajo Gospel Mission, an independent mission, at Hardrock, Arizona, in 1932. Other missions were started in the 1940's: Saunders Bible Mission at Houck in 1941, Pine Haven Baptist in 1947, Bisti Methodist School in 1947, Star Lake Bible Mission in 1947, Twin Buttes and Smoke Signal Nazarene Missions in 1947. In 1940, Howard Clark started an indigenized church at Crystol and put in charge six elders. Attendance averaged sixty people.

Navajo pastors were scarce during this period of time. Churches were dominated by Anglos, paternalism was the order of the day, and mission compounds grew larger with diversified programs. Most Christians were from the lowest economic level or the products of mission schools and very few came from the latter source.[2] In times of crisis and trouble nearly all Navajo Christians would go back to the medicine man.

Churches had large attendance at Christmas, Easter and Thanksgiving when food, gifts and other material inducements attracted large crowds; but born again Christians, incorporated into local churches and witnessing to other Navajos, were few and far between.

In 1950, after fifty years of missionary effort, the following results in terms of number of churches planted can be noted. Each of these denominations, in addition, had several preaching points.

Presbyterian.............. 7 churches
Methodists................ 1 church
Christian Reformed........12 churches
Episcopalian.............. 6 churches
American Baptist.......... 1 church
*Nazarene................. 2 churches
**Independent missions....... 6 churches

* Nazarenes began planting churches in the late
  1940's
** Emmanuel Missions was started in 1922; Navajo
   Bible School and Mission in 1938; The Crystol
   Church in 1938; The Good News Mission in 1941;
   Navajo Gospel Mission in 1932; Star Lake Bible
   Mission in 1947.

1950 Altogether there were no more than 35 organized
congregations with resident pastors. Only one or two
had a Navajo pastor.   In the next 27 years, 308 new
churches would be planted with resident pastors, and
203 of these pastors would be Navajo.

THE 27 UNBELIEVABLE YEARS
1950-1977

In the 1950's there was no great increase in
number of Christians or organized churches, but there
was a great influx of missions and missionaries due
in part to national awareness of the Navajo.

It was not the missionary that made the Navajos
receptive. It was the breaking down of their old religion, resulting in cracks in the cohesion of the
culture, calling for cultural change.

As one Navajo pastor puts it:

When they say to me the missionary has
destroyed the old religion, I say no, it was
not the missionary. It was the wine bottle,
the *bich'ah lichíí'íí*. When you drank it and
fell in your hoghan upon your medicine bag,
the power left you (conversation with J.
Thompson, August, 1977).

To the Navajo, education, science, and man walk-
ing on the moon (a sacred god) all helped destroy the
credibility of the old religion. The mythology of the

culture was no longer believable to many.

From the years 1950 to 1977, the following congregations were planted:

Assembly of God..............32 congregations
Baptists.....................61 congregations
Brethren..................... 6 congregations
Independent Christian Churches
                             6 congregations
Presbyterian................. 4 congregations
Christian Reformed.......... 8 congregations
Church of Christ............. 7 congregations
Christiam Missionary Alliance
                             1 congregation
           (2 more in the process)
Episcopalian................. 4 congregation
Friends...................... 3 congregations
Evangelical Lutheran......... 3 congregations
Mennonite.................... 6 congregations
Methodists................... 2 congregations
Wesleyan and Free Methodists. 8 congregations
Nazarene.....................15 congregations
Indigenous Pentecostals......76 congregations
           (6 more in the process)
Pentecostal Holiness.........24 congregations
Navajo Gospel Mission........ 8 congregations
Non-denominational...........30 congregations
Seventh Day Adventists....... 4

Mission Schools

Mission schools have produced many leaders for
the schools and the tribe but only a few for the
church at large on the Navajo Reservation.

It is obvious that mission schools for whatever
reason, have not fulfilled their intent of supplying
a force to evangelize the Navajo Nation. If they do
not have a viable program for producing Navajo church
leadership and planting churches, what is their purpose? They provide a place for Christian Navajo families to send their children where they can be educated in a Christian atmosphere.   There is an increasing cry for this schooling opportunity from Navajo
parents. Mission schools must gear their programs to
meet this need.

Other and different programs must be developed

to produce leadership for the churches.

Where have the pastors on the Navajo Reservation come from? Eighty to ninety percent of Navajo pastors have received their training on the job. Special training courses have supplemented basic apprenticeship training.

Indigenous Pentecostal churches have produced 73 pastors for their churches almost entirely through an apprenticeship system. They learn by assisting a veteran evangelist or pastor. Most pastors on the Reservation have no formal college or seminary training. Only a few have attended a Bible Training School.

One new suggested program for training leadership is Theological Education by Extension, or TEE. In addition, short seminars for training pastors,that do not disrupt their ministry or remove them from their communities for long extended periods of time, need to be held periodically across the Reservation.

Indigeneity is a factor motivating Navajo men to become pastors. Navajo men will not respond to the call to feed the flock of God where the church is dominated by Anglos.

Indigenous Pentecostal churches have 73 Navajo pastors and no Anglo pastors. Denominational Pentecostal churches have 19 Anglo pastors and only two Navajo pastors. The basic difference in these two groups is that one is indigenous from its inception and the other is Anglo dominated. There is little difference in doctrine or style of service.

The "Navajo Church must develop a sense of selfhood[3]. if there is to be spontaneous growth and then leadership will rise to the top "as cream rises on milk."[4].

The Growing Church

The multiplication of missions and churches has caused the Navajo to be labeled "the most missionaried people in the world" (Christianity Today,May 9, 1975, 46). The label may be accurate, but it needs to be pointed out that in the last 27 years, 203 Navajo began pastoring churches and Anglo pastors number only 120. Many other missionaries work in supportive ministries.

Not only has the number of congregations, now numbering 343 with 12,395 Navajo attending church regularly, increased dramatically but the quality of Christians has risen beyond belief. No longer can it be said that Navajo in time of crisis always retreat to the medicine man. A number of these new Christians are a result of the large increase of camp churches.

A deeper reason for these new quality Christians is the result of the work of the Holy Spirit in the lives of the Navajo. After years of planting and watering God is giving the increase. Jesus said, I will build My Church.

Jesus is no respecter of denominations or human organizations, although in history He has used them mightily and discarded them when these human structures have become an end in themselves. He has built His Church on the Navajo Reservation using committed individuals and structures and raising up new individuals and structures when His objectives require. Some of the new structures he is using to build His Church on the Reservation are discussed elsewhere in this book.

NOTES

1. At Ft. Defiance, men like J. D. Perkins in 1880 were assigned by the Presbyterian Home Mission to teach in the newly built government school. From 1880-1897 the government Indian policy was one of employing missionary personnel as school teachers (Terrell 1970: 250).

2. According to research of Dr. Alan Tippett in 1960's (unpublished notes).

3. See article on church structure and self-hood.

4. cf. Herman Williams, taped speech at Rock Point Lutheran Mission, November, 1976.

BIBLIOGRAPHY

BEETS, HENRY
  1940 Toiling and Trusting Grand Rapids
         Printing Co., Grand Rapids, Mich.

DEKORNE, J. C.
  1947 Navajo and Zuni for Christ Christian
         Reformed Board of Missions Publ.,
         Grand Rapids, Mich.

MALEHORN, PAULINE
  1948 The Tender Plant manuscript published
         at Navajo Methodist Mission, Farmington,
         N.M.

MEANS, FLORENCE GRANELL
  1955 Sagebrush Surgeon Friendship Press, N.Y.

McDONALD, ELEANOR D. and JOHN B. ARRINGTON
  1971 The San Juan Basin: My Kingdom was a
         County Green Mountain Press, Denver, CO

OPPENHUIZEN, ED and JOHN KLEIN
  n.d. A Brief Introduction for New Workers on
         the Indian Mission Field n.p., mimeo

SALSBURY, CLARENCE G., M.D.
  1969 The Salsbury Story The University of
         Arizona Press, Tucson, AZ

SALSBURY, CORA B.
  n.d. Forty Years in the Desert: A History of
         Ganado Mission 1901-1940 n.p.

SMITH, RICHARD K. and J. MELVIN NELSON
  1969 Date Lines and Bylines, A Sketch Book of
         Presbyterian Beginnings and Growth in
         Arizona Synod of Arizona, USA publisher

  -------- Southwest Bible and Missionary Conference
             Seventieth Anniversary Publication n.d.,
             n.a., n.p., Flagstaff

Interviews

CLARK, ALMA and DAVID CLARK at Navajo Bible School and Mission, June, 1977, Window Rock, AZ.

OLDMAN, GRACE from author's field notes, Red Mesa, AZ, 1969.

4
Church Structures Among the Navajo

The early Protestant mission work among the
Navajo followed the traditional pattern of Indian
missions. It may be added that, according to
R. Pierce Beaver, the pattern for both home and foreign missions was set in early American Indian
missions (1966:62).

THE COMPOUND CHURCHES

This was to set up a compound in which the missionaries and their national helpers would live in
isolation from the indigenous population. Schools
were established to educate the children so that they
might receive religious instruction, be able to read
the Bible, and become good civilized Christians. At
the same time, evangelistic efforts were carried on
and a chapel was built on the compound in order that
converts might worship God.

On the Navajo Reservation, this type of mission
church has been established by the Presbyterians, the
Christian Reformed, Methodist, Brethren in Christ, as
well as a couple of non-denominational missions. All
of these missions, however, have trained Navajo pastors and have established outstations. The compound
church does not seem to have been successful in any
instance. They are usually attended by the Navajos
who are employed by the mission with a few people
from outside. The missionaries are predominant, even
though they may try to avoid being so. The Navajo
just do not take the lead, though they may do at
least half the preaching. Somehow, they have the

underlying attitude that this is the white man's show
and they are merely employed helpers.

THE MISSION ESTABLISHED CHURCHES

[The outstations provide more freedom and more
opportunity to work directly with the people of the
community. As a result, these have shown more growth
on the whole.] There is not the school, clinic and
other activities to sap the time and energy of the
pastor. Some of these outstations have a resident
missionary along with the pastor and some do not have
a Navajo pastor. In the latter case, the local Christian men may serve as interpreters.

This same pattern usually applies to the many
denominational and independent churches which have
come more recently and have not established schools
and hospitals. These include Baptist, Mennonite,
Assemblies of God, Nazarene, etc., each with their
own particular emphasis. Both the mission compound
churches and the outstation type churches have been
involved in a great deal of paternalism. The giving
of used clothing, Christmas give-away services, and
so on, has tended to elevate the missionary to the
place of benefactor. The people usually come for
services of one kind or another and tend to put the
missionary in the role of benefactor.

Services in the vast majority of these churches
are patterned after the particular denominational
service of the dominant culture. The order of service, singing of translated hymns (which can't be un-
derstood by uninitiated Navajos), beginning with the
doxology and ending with the benediction, etc., is
just like a church in Pasadena. There are some excep-
tions to the rule as some have departed from this
rigid structure to a greater or lesser extent, especially when the white man's influence has been re-
moved.

THE INDIGENOUS CAMP CHURCHES

In the following discussion, we will look at one
church that has been established on Black Mesa by a
Navajo pastor under the support and direction of the
Navajo Gospel Mission and another at Red Mesa which
was started by a Christian Church missionary and
allowed to develop indigenously. Both of these are

indigenous churches;   the Black Mesa Church is very
Navajo and is growing along kinship lines, the Red
Mesa Church does incorporate much of the Navajo cul-
ture and is growing in two Clan groups.

The Black Mesa Church

The Black Mesa Church is in a remote area and
most of the people live according to the traditional
Navajo way of life.   Through the efforts of Bruce
Yazzie, a Navajo evangelist, a nuclear family
(Cranks) became Christians.   Paul Johnson, a young
man from the Cactus Valley area also became a
Christian and later attended the Bible training
classes at Navajo Gospel Mission. A marriage was ar-
ranged between Paul and Thelma, a girl from the Crank
family, and as is the custom, Paul went to live at
his wife's home. He had some further training at the
mission and experience in preaching and witnessing at
Sand Springs. He then requested to be allowed to work
with his own (wife's) people at Black Mesa.   While
still receiving his salary from the mission, he moved
into the family camp and there began having services
and visiting in the area. [Most of the people in the
area were kin relatives, so he and Thelma were *missn-*
welcome. It is very difficult for a Navajo to visit *worker*
people who are not related, as this just isn't done.] *should*
They want to know, "Why did you come to me?" and the *be*
inference is, "Why did you come here not being a rel- *related.*
ative of mine."

Even though he was employed by the mission, Paul
was expected to do his share of the family work.   He
was expected to herd sheep, haul wood and water and
use his pick-up to take family members to the trading
post.   This created some tension, but it was re-
solved when Paul took a job at the coal mine and went
off the mission payroll. As he continued to work with
the people, other families in the extended family began to respond.   Services were conducted in a very
informal way, always with a meal afterwards much like
a Navajo ceremony. This church has continued to grow
both in number and in spiritual maturity. Problems
over land, livestock, etc., that would have been
dealt with in the chapter house are now taken care of
in the church. If Paul was unable to find the answer

in the Bible, he would often look for help from the
senior pastor (Bruce Yazzie) at the mission. This
church is operating within the traditional Navajo social structure and it is interesting to observe how
they find Christian functional substitutes for traditional religious functions. I witnessed a feast in
honor of the baby's first laugh, held at the Black
Mesa Church. The form was that of the traditional
ceremony, but the meaning was changed to that of
Christian dedication, which included prayer for the
baby and its parents. Most of the extended family
members in the area are now Christians and they are
planning evangelism in the area to the south.

The Red Mesa Church

The church at Red Mesa grew very slowly at
first. There was an attempt to incorporate the items
of Navajo culture which were felt to be compatible
with Christianity into these early services. In 1966
they began having services in hoghans and continued
in this manner for three years. During this time
there were no converts until August of 1969, when a
family of five people came to the Lord. These five
were a 95 year old medicine man, his wife, a son-in-
law, a daughter and a stepson.[1]
    In the fall of 1972, Jim Charley, a Navajo man,
was converted from a life of dissipation and drinking
through an Indian mission in Phoenix, Arizona. A year
later, in 1973, he moved back to the Reservation as a
man dedicated and committed to being a "missionary"
to his own people. His parents were part of the Red
Mesa Church. Jim started preaching for this church
as soon as he moved to Red Mesa in 1973, but the
church did not grow at this point.
    In 1974, the meeting place for the Red Mesa
Church was changed from the mission to the home of
Jim Charley's mother and stepfather. This was also
the location of Jim's trailer house in which his immediate family lived. After this move, Jim Charley
became the accepted pastor of the Red Mesa Church and
another Navajo man, Harvey Yazzie, became his assist-
ant. The role of the missionary greatly decreased
and that of these men greatly increased during the
year. Services were started in the homes of Christian

families in four other locations.

Those proven and effective elements that were compatible with the culture and not forbidden by the Bible were adopted. The white missionary had added multi-individual praying and regular tent meetings (four to six meetings a year) and praying for the sick. Jim Charley and Harvey Yazzie added laying on of hands, annointing with oil, playing drums, amplified guitar music and large loud speakers for the preacher and song leader.

While these two growing churches are radically different in many respects, *both are characterized by strong Navajo leadership and identity*. The Red Mesa's emphasis on healing could be an important element for growth in Navajo society.

These two churches meet important Navajo felt needs and concepts of indigeneity. They provide a sense of self-hood. (Tippett, 1973: 154)

First of all, they meet the need for self determination. In a day when the Navajo people are insisting on self determination in government, it makes little sense to deny them the control of their churches. The Navajo tribe is now called The Navajo Nation and this is proudly displayed on vehicles and on letterheads. There is a growing impatience on the part of Navajo Christian leaders who have been denied the opportunity to oversee autonomous congregations. The camp church provides this opportunity and the Navajo Christians have demonstrated both their capability and their desire for self determination.

There is also the need for self respect or self pride in the good sense. This comes from a job well done, a feeling that one owns something of which he is proud or has attained success in an undertaking. Herman Williams, a Navajo pastor at Navajo Mountain expressed it in the following statement made at a Church Growth Conference at Rock Point, Arizona. "Indians have feelings just as the white man has feelings; you've got to think how I feel, how my congregation feels as Indians. The white man thinks, 'These poor Indians, they don't know anything, they can't paint, they can't work,' and so they bring outsiders to do the work." He shows further how the people weave baskets to pay for their butane bills. The people then have the satisfaction of knowing that

they are taking care of their church.   If all the
work is done by outsiders, the Indian figures that
this is not his church. In the camp church the people
take care of their own buildings and conduct their
own services and evangelistic efforts and have a
sense of pride in what God is doing through them.

The Navajo camp church meets another basic need,
that of self-identity. Here a group of Navajo people
are members of a thoroughly Navajo church within
their own social structure. Here a person is sur-
rounded by his or her own kin folk and is aware that
he does not have to become an Anglo to be a good
Christian. These folk can feel free to criticize the
white man's ways and often do. There is no sense that
they are practicing a foreign religion; in fact the
adoption of a number of functional substitutes gives
their worship a distinctive Navajo flavor.   The on-
slaught of the dominant culture over the years where
the design has often been to "civilize" the Indian
(which meant the destruction of their cultures) has
been devastating to their identity. It has often resulted in demoralization evidenced in alcoholism and
other symptoms of despair.

Christians in every land are proud of their cultural and national background. They believe that being a Christian makes them a better Swede, Korean or
American.   The Navajo wants to feel the same way.
(Praise God that there are churches that enable
people to feel that they are better Navajos.)

NOTES

1. Conversion is described in article on conversion
   process.

BIBLIOGRAPHY

BEAVER, R. PIERCE
    1966   Church State and the American Indian.
           Missouri: Concordia.

TIPPETT, A. R.
    1973   Verdict Theology in Missionary Theory.
           California: Pasadena. William Carey
           Library.

5
Navajo Church Growth: Contributing Factors

⌐One of the basic reasons for the study of Navajo
churches was to try to gain some insight that would
help us produce growing churches. This article deals
with the more obvious factors that seem to contribute
to growth and non-growth in churches.⌐

*Churches are growing that have the right kind of
leadership.* Leadership that inspires the confidence
of the people. Navajo and Anglo pastors must exhibit
quite different qualities of leadership.

The Navajo pastor must be authoritative without
being dictatorial. He must not be apologetic about
his education, Biblical knowledge, competence to organize and run a church. He must have a clear knowledge of the Bible that impresses both the schooled
and unschooled. *(All adult Navajos are educated, but
not all have had Western schooling.)*

Anglo pastors *(and several larger churches have
Anglo pastors)* must not be authoritative. They must
openly exhibit large quantities of love - the fruit
of the Spirit. In the pulpits they must speak as
though they utter the oracles of God. They must be
responsive to the counsel and the felt needs of the
people.

⌐*Churches are growing that meet the felt needs of
the people.*⌐1. Different groups have different felt
needs and, while the Navajo are very much one people
and one tribe, they are in different stages of acculturation and economic development and thus have different felt needs. Different kinds of churches are
growing in different areas. In developing towns such

as Crownpoint, Shiprock, Window Rock, Ft. Defiance,
Tuba City, Chinle and Kayenta, the Navajo are moving
into housing developments. They are being urbanized
and no longer live next to their relatives; their
neighbors may be strangers. This change in housing
patterns and social structure has ramifications
throughout the life way of these people. There are
new felt needs: the need for community, the need to
belong, the need to learn English and the need to
learn to read Navajo, the need for friends, the need
for supernatural power to meet daily spiritual and
physical needs. In this culture, the church that is
not supernatural is superficial. It is only by daily
contact with these people that a pastor can know and
minister to these felt needs. Pastors that lack daily
contact on a face to face basis and involvement with
the struggles of these people will never be able to
minister to their felt needs. Their preaching will be
content-centered rather than people-centered.

*[Churches are growing that are working within a
single homogeneous unit.]* All Navajo are being acculturated, but at differing rates. In Shiprock, New
Mexico, there are C-1, C-2, C-3 and C-4 Navajo (C
stands for culture or acculturation).

C-4 Navajos are strongly nationalistic and vocal
for Indian culture. Some are well-educated. They are
acculturated, but are moving away from Anglo-culture.
Many of them are militant and anti-Christian; some
are members of A.I.M. They are not receptive at this
time.

C-3 Navajos are bi-cultural and operating effectively in two cultures. Some are more at home in the
Anglo culture and are assimilating with it. They almost never live in camps. They prefer English to
Navajo. They dress in suits for church and office.
They are called *bilasasnas* ("apples" -red on the outside and white on the inside) by the C-1 Navajo.

C-2 Navajo are rapidly becoming acculturated,
but are more at home in the Navajo culture. They long
to improve their lot educationally and economically
and will attend English services even when they do
not understand because they want to learn English. By
and large, they dress and remain in full contact with
most aspects of Navajo culture. They are highly

receptive at this time to a church that meets their felt needs.⌋

C-1 Navajo are mildly anti-Anglo; at least very selective in their white friends. They almost all live in camps. If they go to church it will be to one where there is a Navajo preacher (one who uses the Navajo language).Many attend revivalistic Pentecostal churches; they know traditional Navajo culture well. If they are not Christian, they are active in traditional Navajo religion or the Peyote movement. They are receptive to the right program.

An acculturation profile might look like this:[2.]

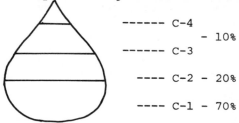

Churches are growing that have the right mixture of ingredients.⌋ No one thing causes a church to grow, but the right mixture of the right ingredients will cause it to grow in the right way just as good cakes must have the right mixture of a number of ingredients. A cake that is all flour is tasteless and one that is all sugar is sickening. Larger churches will grow across kinship lines, providing there is a proper mixing of the right ingredients. Some of these ingredients are: a receptive homogeneous people, emphasis on the supernatural power available to Christians, proper attention to the rate of acculturation in the group, meeting felt needs, providing instruction for the entire family (not just adults or just children), the right kind of pastoral leadership, the right kind of lay leadership, fitting the type of service to the type of homogeneous unit, e.g. C-3, C-2, C-1 Navajo.⌋

In surveying churches on the Reservation, we attended three growing churches and three non-growing churches in Shiprock, New Mexico. The three growing churches were quite different from each other for

each was growing in a different homogeneous unit. The
three non-growing churches lacked one or more of the
ingredients necessary to church growth in this community.
     Two of the non-growing churches had Anglo pas-
tors.   The services were in English with interpreters.   One church used earphones and the interpreter
was in a secluded room translating the message as
fast as it was preached.   The congregation, however,
was mixed - half non-Navajo and half Navajo. Sixty
were present.   The church has been there thirty plus
years and has not grown for some time.   One ingredi-
ent missing in this church was an emphasis on supernatural power available to Christians.   The service
fit the Anglo half of the congregation better than
the Navajo.   The Navajo attending were adults, all
over forty, and very small children.   The church was
not reaching the large number of people in the 15-35
age group.   (These 15-35 are a rapidly acculturating
group and the largest age group of Navajo.)   Any
church that is not reaching this age group is not
growing.   This church and others like it are cut off
from effectively reaching the masses of C-1 Navajo
because their services are geared for C-3 Navajo.They
would have to use a Navajo pastor to reach more C-1
people.
     The other non-growing church in Shiprock is in-
digenous, but lacks a program for all ages.   The program of the church is mostly "revival" meetings that
are well-attended, but regular services are adult-
oriented only.   There is no program for children and
young people.   Many of these "revivalistic," pentecostal churches exist on the Reservation and need
help in establishing a program for all ages. An Anglo
working with a C-1 pastor must not be domineering for
it is important for a church among C-1 Navajo to have
a Navajo pastor fully in charge.
     The growing churches included one of C-1 Navajo
and two of C-2 Navajo.   The first meets in a house
that has been expanded by the addition of a large
tent-like shelter built onto the house.   This congregation was started in October 1976 and has over a
hundred in attendance every Sunday. The preacher is a
strong leader who is a well known "revivalist" on the

Reservation. He preaches regularly for this congregation and for two others, traveling 150 miles every
Sunday. He also speaks nightly in tent meetings. The
service includes indigenous musical instruments -drum
and guitars, a lot of audience participation, long
services, lots of testimonies, and is largely adult
oriented. The Sunday I was there, pickups lined the
narrow streets of this unplanned part of town. Rapid
growth is due to the dramatic leadership of the
preacher and because the service fits the homogeneous
unit. The service is all in Navajo except singing,
which includes English songs and choruses, although
the preacher is highly educated and fluent in both
languages. There is much emphasis on miracles and
healing.

A second growing church runs 200 in attendance.
It has an adult English Sunday School class with an
Anglo teacher (23 present), and an adult class in
Navajo with 33 present, about 40 teenagers and 90
children in a well developed Sunday School. The pastor is a Navajo who is a strong leader. He is well
educated with strong principles and convictions. He
is a community leader and member of the school board.
The church is C-2 with some C-3 people. Younger
couples dress in suits and Western dresses. The
church emphasizes the supernatural power for the
Christian's life and the pastor brings relevant, in-
tellectually stimulating and emotionally penetrating
messages. One Sunday, when I was there, he covered
in his sermon Ephesians 4:8, "When He ascended on
High, He led captive a host of captives." He explained that when Christ was in the grave He bound
all our enemies, (spiritual powers) that had before
bound us. Jesus bound our spiritual enemies while in
the grave, and when He ascended He kept them captive
so that we might have power to resist them - a bit of
ethnotheology that Western preachers would never have
deduced, but helpful to Navajo. This church emphasizes redemption and lift - not lift via social services, but lift from redemption (McGavran,1970:p.260)
and a new life in Christ that results in better jobs,
opportunities, etc. They attempt to win people who
are economically successful as well as all strata of
society so that young Navajo will be able to find
success images in the church and know that they can

become successful also.

The third growing church is pastored by an Anglo. It has a Sunday School that meets at 9:00 AM with 75 to 100 children attending and no adults. The children are bussed home and another service is held at 10:00 AM. This service is all in English and the church fills to capacity with 120 to 140 adults and very few children. This service is very Western and many young couples attend this service. They dress in everyday Navajo dress, there are many teenagers and some older Navajo, only two or three Anglos. An overhead projector is used for putting new English songs on the screen and to illustrate the sermon. Even Navajo who do not speak much English come to this service because they like the Anglo pastor and they want to learn English. Nothing is done in Navajo. Songs are old traditional Western hymns. The message, however, is well preached using passages from the church's catechism and from the Scripture; it covered major Biblical themes and was applied to the Christian life, offering him supernatural power in meeting daily spiritual needs. It also meets the intellectual needs of those coming into Western education. The pastor is not domineering. He told me that he was sent by his denomination to the Reservation because he "lacked leadership." He exerts a beautiful kind of leadership that counts others as better than himself. He speaks the Word of God forcefully. His greatest asset is his abounding love for his people. He embraces them in church, especially when they have made an important commitment. He exhibits the fruit of the Spirit - love. The people know he is genuine and not ethnocentric.

It was amazing to me to see the success of this Anglo pastor. He taught me that it requires a different type of leadership if you are an Anglo pastor than if you are a Navajo pastor. The Navajo pastor needs to be somewhat authoritative. The Anglo pastor needs to lead without dominating the church. He must continually seek the counsel of his Navajo leaders. This church is composed of C-2 people who are on the way up economically. The church is the oldest in Shiprock, but only ran twenty adults in attendance

eight years ago when this pastor first came. At that
time there were few in the church of ages 15-35, but
now there are many.[3].

In addition, this church has an all-Navajo service at 11:00 AM. This service is led by the Navajo
pastor and nothing is done in English in this service; about 45 attend. In many areas where C-2 Navajo
live in developing communities it would be good to
have an all-English service and an all-Navajo service
to meet the needs of two different groups of people.
This also gets rid of the lengthy service where
everything is said in both Navajo and English. Altogether in the three services of Sunday morning,
February 13, 1977, there were over 250 different men,
women and children attending this congregation.

We hope from the above descriptions that it can
be seen that church growth over an area requires the
right mixture of many ingredients with a different
combination for each homogeneous unit.   To find the
right mixture requires wisdom, discernment, cultural
sensitivity and receptiveness to the leading of the
Holy Spirit, whose chief business is growing and mul-
tiplying churches.

Churches are growing that solidly incorporate
their members. In Pentecostal churches, people are
baptized by an evangelist after a big meeting rather
than by the local churches, and the converts do not
know where their congregation is located.   They follow the evangelist for awhile, then quit; they have
no sense of belonging.

Evangelicals who fail to teach and baptize
people who have made a decision and incorporate them
solidly into local congregations settle for little
growth, when there could have been major growth.
Church growth depends on incorporating those who are
won into local congregations where they are conserved, strengthened and sent forth.

Churches are growing that do not confuse "ser-
vice" with "mission." If you do not aim at the target, you are not likely to hit it. If the target is
church growth, then anything short of that has missed
the target.   Churches whose goal it is to make disciples (Matthew 28:19,20) and plant churches that
"continue steadfastly in the Apostles' doctrine,

fellowship, breaking of bread and prayer,"(Acts 2:42)
do not confuse service with mission. There is a place
for service, but service does not become mission.
Missions that have all kinds of service projects to
help the Navajo are to be commended for their social
concern, but if one rationalizes that these service
projects are somehow going to help make disciples and
plant churches, then that mission is following an il-
lusion. Service projects can be justified, but they
cannot be justified as substitutes for evangelism.
Quite to the contrary, they pull away financial and
man power resources that could be deployed for church
growth. *The denominations that are growing best and
planting the most churches are not using service
projects to do it.* They are aiming for the target
and hitting it with considerable success, and service
projects come as effects or results of growth.

Our observations were that some churches are not
growing:

    a. Racially integrated churches are not
       growing.
    b. Ingrown churches are not growing.
    c. Churches composed of people over 40
       and little children with very few
       between the ages of 15 and 35 are
       not growing.
    d. Churches that are not ministering to
       the entire family are not growing.
       Navajo will go to church where their
       children want to go. No active Sun-
       day school or youth program means no
       growth.

NOTES

1. For discussion of felt needs, see Chapter 6.
2. Adapted from Alan Tippett's economic model into an
   acculturation model.
3. Interview, February 13, 1977.

6

Navajo Evangelism:
Scratching Where It Itches

"The Spirit of the Lord is upon me, because he hath anointed me to preach the Gospel to the poor; he hath sent me to heal the brokenhearted, to preach deliverance to the captives, and recovering of sight to the blind, to set at liberty them that are bruised,to preach the acceptable year of the Lord" (Luke 4:18-19). With these words from the prophetic scriptures, Jesus announced His ministry to the people in the synagogue in Nazareth. It was *good news to the poor, healing to the brokenhearted, deliverance to the captives, sight to the blind, liberty to the oppressed.* In other words, Jesus came with a ministry and a message that met the felt needs of people.

A fundamental truth from both communication theory and decades of evangelistic experience is that people ignore messages that do not speak to their *felt needs* and levels of understanding (Engle, 1976; 94). Too often our presentation of the Biblical message has missed the mark because of our failure to understand the target audience. This happens when we have not made an effort to know the people, their aspirations, values and frustrations. Participation by missionaries in the indigenous life-way has been all too rare and few know what the felt needs of the people are.

It should be pointed out that felt needs are psychological in nature. They are needs that are really *felt* by the individual. The felt need may be on a conscious or a sub-conscious level. Programs are

often initiated to meet the needs of a group of
people for better housing, sanitation and good nutri-
tion. These programs may fail not because the needs
do not exist, but because the people do not *feel* the
need for such things. Many people, for instance, are
unaware that they have a deep longing for meaning and
purpose in life until they find it in Christ. Then
they testify that Christ met the deepest need of
their life in giving them a reason for living.

Sometimes these sub-conscious felt needs are
brought to the level of awareness by a very vocal
member of the group or by educational processes. A
case in point would be the recent emphasis on the
self-image of young Indians. This has resulted in a
number of ways including movements like A.I.M. Whether implicit or explicit, felt needs are needs that
leave a vacuum within the heart.

Repeatedly, perceptive, spirit-filled evangelists, aware of the felt needs of people, have reaped
a great harvest. Pastors living close to their congregations become aware of their problems and desires
and carry out an effective ministry of spiritual
healing and inspiration. Others, aloof in their ivory
towers, offer stones in the place of bread and fail
to apply the healing balm to wounded spirits.

The purpose of this article is to stress the importance of knowing the target audience, the Navajo
people, and to apply the Gospel to the areas of felt
needs. We will be looking at some broad areas of
felt needs as the writer sees them. It is hoped that
someone more qualified will do a more thorough study.
It should be obvious that individuals, as well as
homogeneous groups differing in age, acculturation,
etc., will have different felt needs.

It is worth noting at this point that people
living in a healthy culture with a tightly knit social structure are typically slow to accept the Gospel. This is because their felt needs are being met
relatively well in most areas of life. But when a
society is in the process of rapid change and the old
assumptions are being questioned, people find themselves in a state of tension and frustration.

The Navajo people today are in the process of
quite rapid acculturation in the direction of the
dominant society and many are aware that the old

supports are no longer there. There are many indica-
tors that the people are actively looking for other
answers and when this attitude prevails, you have a
ripening harvest field.

This article is dealing with the relationship of
felt needs to Navajo evangelism. We have come to the
conclusion that the most effective strategy for evan-
gelizing the Navajo people is the multiplication of ✓
churches.[1] While outreach programs such as vacation
Bible schools and camp visitation are both necessary
and helpful, it is the regular church services and
evangelistic meetings that are most effective in making disciples. Every aspect, however, of our evangelistic outreach needs to be based on the felt needs
of the people. This is especially true of the use of
the media. I am convinced that the thoughtful use of
radio and television will greatly enhance the overall
evangelistic ministry of the churches.

The fact that a large number of the churches are
family churches located right in the camp, the center
of Navajo communal life, makes them a very visible
witness to Christianity. Non-Christian relatives attend services regularly and have the opportunity to
make an evaluation in terms of their own felt needs.

People also attend churches in the developing
communities such as Shiprock. These people are usually more acculturated younger Navajos, many of whom
are driven by deep inner needs to search for help or
relief. The churches that are aware of these felt
needs and are aiming their messages aright will
attract these hungry people.

Our study of Navajo churches points up strongly
that growing churches are need-meeting churches. The
question we should ask, then, is, "What should we emphasize in our churches in order to touch the areas
of Navajo felt needs?"

SOCIAL NEEDS

Like any other people, Navajo have social needs.
These include a sense of belonging, mutual aid and
recreation. Most social interaction takes place in
the extended family in the day to day existence. This
is the basic cooperating group in meeting physical
needs and in putting on religious ceremonies. Other

opportunities for social intercourse are provided by
the larger ceremonies such as the Squaw Dance (ndáá')
and Yéii Bichei Dances. Visits to the trading posts,
chapter meetings and sheep dips provide opportunities
for sharing news and gossip. As Kluckhohn points out,
"Navajos love to have a good time. As is natural for
isolated people, the greatest pleasure lies in an occasion which brings crowds together." (1962:96)
        The Navajo churches then should provide for good
fellowship. One of the greatest weaknesses in missions among the Navajos is that there has often been
no provision for fellowship. Decisions have been recorded at camp meetings, Christmas programs and other
special meetings, but little thought has been given
to the plight of the convert. He must return to the
family camp to live the Christian life without fellowship or encouragement. Where does this Christian
now belong? ⌊To take a firm stand for Christ is to
cut oneself off from the social functions of the family, yet there is no local church which will provide
a functional substitute for these activities.   He
feels like a social outcast when the other members
ask him to help with the ceremonies and he must refuse because of his Christian convictions.⌋
        It is expected that a disciple of Christ should
suffer persecution and rejection for his Lord, but
the church is God's provision for encouragement, belonging and edification. Providing a church fellowship, however small, will go a long way to meeting
these needs. ⌈Otherwise, as the statistics show, the
chances for regression are great.⌋ This is why evangelism does not end with decision, but with incorporation into a body of believers. The very fact that a
church exists in a community, then, is an answer to
the felt need of fellowship and belonging.
        The next question to ask is, "Does this church
provide a quality fellowship that is satisfying socially and that will attract Navajo people?"
It should be a caring fellowship.
        If it is a family church (which the majority
are) this will be taken care of automatically in the
kinship cooperating patterns.   Much emphasis on the
Christian teaching of love for one another will add a
dimension to this that will attract non-Christians.

It would be a striking witness in a community to see Christians help one another in practical ways. Emphasis should be placed on praying for one another by name.

It should be an active fellowship
    Growing churches among Navajos are active churches. It is not enough to schedule the Sunday service and the Wednesday night prayer meeting. Plan lots of camp meetings, pot-lucks, evangelistic meetings and other special activities. The Christian will have a real social need met and others will come to "see what's going on." Remember, Navajo society is a feasting society!

It should be a joyful fellowship
    Stress the joy of being a Christian and the victorious aspects of the Christian life. Staid, formal services are not very attractive to Navajo people. There should be ample time for testimonies and singing. Don't be afraid of "Praise the Lord" and "Amen, brother." Pentecostal people don't have a monopoly on these joyful expressions. Remember that worshiping God should be a joyful experience. People should enjoy going to church.

PSYCHOLOGICAL NEEDS

    This is the area that needs much research, but the following are some felt needs that one often observes or hears expressed.

Relief from fear
    An inordinate fear of the dead, witchcraft and taboo is still prevalent among the people. There is much in the Bible that meets this need. Put emphasis on this provision in Christ. If we can say, "The Lord is my Shepherd," we can also say, "Yea, though I walk through the valley of death I will fear no evil, for thou art with me." (Psalm 23) Jesus said, "Greater is He that is in you, than He that is in the world." (I John 4:4) "The Lord is my helper, I will not fear what man can do unto me." (Hebrews 13:6)

Poor self-image
    This has come about as a result of defeat and subjection. The message has come across for many years, implicitly and explicitly, that Navajo people and their ways are inferior. The Biblical message of

God's creation and redemption emphasizes the worth of
all people.   "Behold what manner of love the Father
hath bestowed upon us, *that we should be called the
sons of God!*"   (I John 3:1)   Emphasize the fact that
to be a good Christian is to be a better Navajo.

Alcohol Addiction
       This is   no doubt   related   to the above.   The
greatest killer of Navajos is alcohol and there is a
great desire on the part of many for relief from this
problem.   Emphasis on the life-changing grace of God
even for the worst alcoholic will attract needy
people. We have several men in our church who have
been delivered from a life of alcoholism.   Preach it!

SPIRITUAL NEEDS
       We are inclined, coming as we do from a culture
with a scientific/materialistic world view, to spend
much time with intellectual arguments for the existence of God. The Navajo people are a spiritual
people. They do not need to be convinced of the reality of the supernatural and they don't question the
reality of God. So don't waste time on the obvious,
rather look for areas that reveal spiritual hunger.

Harmony
       Harmony might be the best term to express the
Navajo religious philosophy. If one is to experience
a sense of well being, the delicate balance between
one's self and the supernatural forces must be maintained. When sickness, misfortune or tragedy strike,
something has gotten out of order and must be "put
back again."   This felt need for harmony can be met
by the message of Reconciliation.   Sin has caused
disharmony and this separated man from God,but Christ
has reconciled us to God by His death.

Power
       Navajos, like other animists, are not about to
give up their gods for some intellectual, theoretical
religion. They are convinced of the reality of spiritual forces and can point to many demonstrations of
their existence. They want a god who is able to meet
their needs. Here the missionary must come to grips
with his own faith - is our God able? Growing churches on the Reservation have emphasized the supernatural aspects of Christianity. The majority of Navajo

ceremonies are for the purpose of healing and the people equate healing with supernatural activity. The fact that healing does not always take place does not shake their faith in their religion. Let us preach a God of <u>Power</u> who keeps, heals, saves and delivers. Dr. Alan Tippett says, "In my anthropological notebooks, I have records of interviews with nationals from Mexico, Guatemala and Navajoland, to Taiwan and Indonesia and Ethiopia,so much so that I am persuaded that the Christ of the animist-conversion experience is a Lord of power." (1972:142)

It is possible for a pastor in Los Angeles to be totally irrelevant in his ministry even though he is an Anglo ministering to Anglos. He may find himself rummaging through his old seminary notes or delivering canned sermons from "So and So's 1927 Book of Sermons." He must know his people, know the Word and know his Lord if he is to touch hearts. It is also possible for the Navajo pastor to deliver second-hand messages that are unrelated to Navajo life and felt needs. Let us dedicate ourselves to the noble task of "scratching where it itches."

NOTES

1. See articles in this publication.

BIBLIOGRAPHY

ENGLE, JAMES F.
    1976 "Church Growth Strategies Plus",
           <u>Evangelical Missions Quarterly</u> Vol. 12,
           No. 2, p.94.

KLUCKHOHN, CLYDE and DOROTHY LEIGHTON
    1962 <u>The Navajo</u>, Doubleday and Company, New
           York.

TIPPETT, ALAN R.
    1972 "Possessing the Philosophy of Animism for
           Christ." in <u>Crucial Issues in Missions
           Tomorrow</u>, Moody.

7
Navajo Conversion Process

THE CONVERSION OF TWO NAVAJO MEDICINE MEN

Pete Greyeyes is a converted Navajo medicine man who lives at Navajo Mountain, Arizona.[1] Before conversion, he became very ill and his body broke out in sores. Outside in the juniper tree owls began gathering, not one or two, but ten to twenty owls. Pete knew that the owls were a sign that someone was witching him. In the Navajo culture, owls can represent one's ancestors coming to warn that sickness or calamity or even death lies ahead. Pete Greyeye's immediate cultural response was to call in another medicine man to sing over him. One was called, then another. He even used his own medicine pouch and prayer songs, but all to no avail.

When his wife and daughter began to have the sores they all became desperate. After talking it over, they decided to go to the Navajo preacher, Herman Williams. They arrived late for church one night just as the service was concluding. Herman was finishing the sermon and at the close of the service he gave an invitation. To his surprise, these late-comers came down the aisle and he had some of the members of the church pray with them. After the service, they lingered around the church and Herman began to talk to them about why they had come. He invited them to his home where they told him all that had been happening to them. Herman prayed for them and explained the Good News about Jesus to them until late into the night. That night the family accepted the Lord Jesus Christ as Saviour. About 2:00 AM or 3:00 AM, as the family got up to leave and go back to their hoghan, Pete Greyeyes turned to Herman and asked him how Jesus was going to get rid of those owls. Herman thought for a minute before answering and then he said, "When you get home tonight I want you to go out under those trees and preach to the owls in the name of Jesus Christ."

Pete Greyeyes got in the pickup and as he was driving home he thought about preaching to the owls. He was a Navajo and had no problem understanding witchcraft, but he wasn't crazy. He couldn't imagine anyone who would go out and preach to owls. He was about to go into the hoghan with his family, when his wife reminded him that he was supposed to go out and preach to the owls. His dear wife would not let him into the hoghan until he did what the preacher told him to do, so Pete Greyeyes went out in the wee hours of the morning and preached a sermon to the owls. The sermon went something like this. "There is no reason for you owls to stay here any longer. You can go on home now, or go wherever you want. There is no reason for any of you to stay here because we belong to Jesus now. I belong to Jesus, my family belongs to Jesus, everything here belongs to Jesus, so there is no reason for you owls to stay. Our hoghan belongs to Jesus, our sheep, our cows and horses, our pickup, everything you can see around here belongs to Jesus. So you can leave now." With that, Pete Greyeyes went into the hoghan and went to sleep. He got up the next morning, went outside and to his surprise the owls were all gone. The owls never returned and the sores all left their bodies.

Pete Greyeyes and his family became members of the church and faithful Christians. He took his medicine bag back to the old medicine man who originally gave it to him. He told the old medicine man about his conversion and explained that the bag helped him at times, but when he really needed help it was powerless.

Pete Greyeyes gives this testimony often on the Reservation and recently he has helped to start a church among his family in one of their hoghans. He became their spiritual leader and a preacher of the Gospel.

The second conversion story comes from the Teec Nos Pos area. Honágháahnii was a ninety-five year old medicine man when he became a Christian in 1969. His son-in-law, Jimmy Lowe, came to a camp meeting that was being held in a brush arbor shelter at Red Mesa, Arizona. Jimmy Lowe had only met the missionary one time when he and his family had brought Honágháahnii to him nearly a year before so the missionary could take the old man to the doctor for them.

Preaching in the brush arbor shelter that day was John Peter Yazzie. At the close of the service that Sunday morning, Jimmy Lowe came to the front and told John Peter that he wanted to become a Christian. Following up on this decision, the missionary went to the home of Jimmy Lowe and at the hoghan found the old medicine man and five other members of the family. He asked the family how many of them wanted to become Christians and three of them said they did;one was already a Christian. The missionary began teaching them about the Lord Jesus Christ and spent the whole week visiting daily in their hoghan and going through the Scriptures with them. To everyone's surprise, at the end of the week the old medicine man wanted to become a Christian. As a result of this visitation, five members of the family were baptized at the San Juan River near the Four Corners area. One had already been baptized by Pentecostals.

About two weeks later, the missionary returned for a visit and found the old medicine man exuberant and bubbling over with joy as he tried to tell the missionary something. A member of the family explained that the day before the family had gone to town leaving Honágháahnii alone at the hoghan. Upon returning in the evening they found him on his sheepskin in much pain. They asked him what he had done to get himself in this condition. His answer was "nothing."

He had walked to the sheep corral to check on the penned sheep a time or two, but as the day progressed he got to feeling bad. They inquired further and said, "You must have done something to cause this." The medicine man replied that he had stayed right at the hoghan and prayed to the river where he was baptized. His family told him that he was a Christian now and that he should only pray to the Lord Jesus. Unable to get relief from his pain, the family took him to a Navajo preacher at Sweetwater named Willis George. The preacher prayed for him to be delivered in Jesus' name, praying with the family perhaps until midnight. That night all of Honágháahnii's pain left him and the next morning he was excitedly trying to tell the missionary about it.

Honágháahnii only lived two more years, but in those two years many of his relatives became Christians. His family taught him to pray to the Lord Jesus and he never again prayed to the river, or the mountains, or any of his old gods. He died in a hoghan on a sheepskin at age ninety-seven and his last prayer request was, "Tell Jesus I want to go home."

These two conversion stories have four elements in common.

1. *They involved multi-individual decisions.* Both families discussed together their predicaments and needs.

In the case of Honágháahnii, an uncle had frozen to death after passing out from drinking on a cold night beside the highway. The family depended heavily on this uncle and there was a void in their lives now for they could find no one to help them in times of need.

As the family periodically discussed their need they decided the missionary and the church might be the answer. One member of the family was already converted and no doubt had a high spiritual reason for wanting to become a member of a church. The other members of the family may not have had such a high spiritual motive.

Multi-individual decisions must be decisions in which a group, no matter how small or large, can easily discuss and take a course of action both individually and collectively with justification that makes sense to the entire group. Multi-individual decisions for Christ are often made by families on the Navajo Reservation.

In the case of Pete Greyeyes, the need of the family was for healing and deliverance from witchcraft, with no thought of the need of forgiveness of

sins and the atoning death of Jesus. But it was a
very real need and one that needed a supernatural
answer. They needed to find a power greater than that
of witchcraft. In their family discussions, they decided it was worth a try to see if the prayers of
this Christian preacher would work. Multi-individual
decisions may not always be made from the highest mo-
tives, but if Christians recognize that these families are trying to have a deep spiritual need met in
their lives they can be used of the Lord to bring the
whole family into a saving knowledge of the Lord
Jesus Christ with the least possible social dislocation.

2. *The second thing that these conversion stories
have in common is that a power encounter occurred in
both instances.* Both families went to Navajo preachers who could deal with their sicknesses. They knew
that if they went to the white missionary he would
not understand, but that the Navajo preacher was
spiritually and theologically able to deal with their
needs. To them, their sicknesses had spiritual and
not physical causes. Navajos distinguish between ill-
nesses that have physical causes and those that are
of spiritual origin. The missionary would not approach this attack of pain or sores on the body with
spiritual power, but with western medical power such
as aspirin. The Navajo preacher's approach was
through power encounter and the sufficiency of Christ
and Christian prayer was once and for all established
in those homes. The old gods of the river and the
powers of witchcraft were no rival for the Great
Physician, the Healer and Deliverer, Jesus Christ.

3. *The third thing these stories have in common is
that these men both disposed of the old fetishes and
religious paraphernalia.* In the case of Pete Greyeyes
they were returned to the original owner, the old medicine man, with a word of testimony about its inef-
fectiveness and about having found something more effective in the Lord Jesus Christ.

4. *A fourth thing both of these families had in common was that they were both baptized and incorporated
into the local church.* They became a part of a fellowship of believers soon after their conversion.
They were able to grow in the Lord within a

fellowship that could nurture them and guide and direct them.

   In both of these instances we are dealing with the conversion of medicine men and their families; however, these same elements are evident in a great percentage of Navajo conversions. The following pages deal with dynamics of the Navajo conversion process and we hope that they will stimulate some innovative approaches to evangelism.

UNDERSTANDING CONVERSION DYNAMICS

   Dr. Alan R. Tippett, in an article entitled *Conversion as a Dynamic Process in Christian Missions* which appears in the April 1977 issue of *Missiology*, has given us an excellent framework within which we can study a people movement.[2].

   He said that he did not set up this scheme as a *of* hypothesis and then test it. It is itself an attempt *course.* to organize existing data. This data was gathered over the years while serving as a missionary anthropologist in the island world of the Pacific.

   Tippett says that the process of change from the old context to the new (in our study it is from a non-Christian to a Christian context) can be thought of in three clearcut, but variable units of time. These units he calls the Period of Awareness, the Period of Decision and the Period of Incorporation.

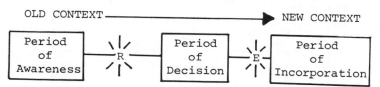

   The diagram shows that there are two specific points that can be identified; the Point of Realization (R) and the Point of Encounter (E).   In order for people to realize the need or desirability to change their needs to be a period in which they are exposed to another way of life, set of values, etc.

   When the point of realization comes, the group enters the Period of Decision. The Period of Decision will vary in time and it may be a decision to accept,

reject or modify the innovation. If they decide to
accept, there is the Point of Encounter when they receive Christ as Lord and Saviour. Then comes the
Period of Incorporation with a break from the old and
an entrance into the new context, usually with some
form of initiation, in the case of Christianity it is
baptism.

Within this context, we will examine the indigenous camp church among the Navajos and its effective-
ness in evangelism. By way of contrast, we will look
at the mission compound approach to evangelism. In
most areas of the Navajo Reservation, the people live
within the traditional social structure and the extended family decision-making process is still in-
tact. We will consider the two types of evangelism
mentioned within each of the three periods and how
they aid or hinder the conversion process.

```
┌───────────────────────────────────────────────┐
│                 MISSION COMPOUND                │
│                                                 │
│   School                                        │
│   Clinic                                        │
│   Used Clothing                                 │
│   Christmas Programs                            │
│   Mechanical and Other Services                 │
│   Burial of Dead                                │
│   - - - - - - - - - - - - - - - - - -           │
│   Mission Church Services                       │
│   Religious Instruction in BIA Schools          │
│   Camp Meetings, VBS, etc.                      │
│   Visitation                                    │
│                   ▼                             │
```

P E R I O D   O F   A W A R E N E S S ⟶ ☀R

```
│                   ▲                             │
│            INDIGENOUS CAMP CHURCH               │
│                                                 │
│   Christian Presence within Society             │
│   Evangelistic Meetings in Camp                 │
│   Meeting of Kinship Obligations                │
│   Functional Substitutes for Former             │
│        Activities                               │
│   Weekly Church Services and Prayer             │
│        Meetings                                 │
│   Bridges Through Marriage Ties To              │
│        Other Camps                              │
└───────────────────────────────────────────────┘
```

It must be pointed out that we are talking about two extremes. There are many churches that would fall on a continuum between the two. It is our observation as a result of the survey that churches whose ministry lies closer to that of the camp church are more effective. Those who are working in developed areas where people are not living within the extended family structure will also find that the principles at work in the camp church apply in large measure to their situation as well. We were surprised to find that the vast majority of churches were predominantly one extended family group, whether within or outside the camp situation.

First of all, then, we must consider how these two approaches contribute to an awareness of Christianity, how they bring Navajo people to the realization of Christianity as a live option and a more satisfying, meaningful way of life than that which they now possess.

The mission compound has been with us since the beginning of modern missions. In fact, this model came out of the early American Indian missions. The typical compound has most of the institutions and activities shown in the diagram. In order to get land it was often necessary to make certain commitments to the tribe, such as education for the children, etc. The main purpose of the mission was to evangelize the people and what better way, it was reasoned, than to instill in young hearts the Word of God. The plight of the people and their need of clothing and medical care prompted other services. As these services increased, more personnel had to be brought in, more buildings erected and as a natural outcome of the Euroamerican love for green things, lawns, trees and flowers sprung up making the compound an oasis in the desert. Thus, the fence around the compound became a wall of partition. The missionaries look out upon the people in their need and sincerely desire to help them, but with a subtle sense of superiority. The Navajo recipients, awed by this strange world, can't help but feel inferior as they ask for help. These acts of kindness in the name of Christ are certainly not wrong in themselves; our Lord taught that we are to love our neighbor. Nor are they without value in

terms of evangelism. People's hearts are often melted
by acts of mercy if done in the right attitude. [Such
"presence" evangelism, however, has a tendency to de-
generate into Paternalism and might even become an
end in itself.]

Most mission compound ministries have direct
"proclamation evangelism." There are the services at
the mission chapel, visitation evangelism, camp meetings and Vacation Bible Schools. In addition to this,
children are taught the Scriptures in the mission
school and at religious instruction classes in the
government boarding schools. In spite of this faithful work, the churches are weak and attendance is
usually small. [Some of these churches have actually
lost ground in recent years.] A goodly number of decisions are usually recorded, but there is a poor
record of conservation. So it seems that this approach has little impact on the people in terms of
moving them toward a meaningful Christian experience.

The Indigenous Camp Church is in some instances
the result of effective outreach from a mission compound.[3]. It is more often a spontaneous development
as a result of Pentecostal evangelistic crusades or
"Revivals." Once a nucleous of believers decides to
have regular meetings in their home camp, the elements
listed in the diagram under Period of Awareness come
into play.

Christians are not gathered out from family and
friends, but continue to live within the group as a
living witness. This is very important for it gives
the non-Christian members of the group an opportunity
to observe Christianity in the milieu of Navajo life.
There is no better way to create an awareness of the
Gospel. The impact becomes greater still when these
believers meet for weekly church services in their
homes and have frequent evangelistic meetings. Family
members often attend these meetings and partake of
the meal that is usually prepared. The Christians
who have separated themselves from the traditional
religious ceremonies thus feel that they have fulfilled their kinship obligations and are not accused
of being stingy for refusing to contribute food and
money for the ceremony. In this respect they are
still considered good Navajos and the fact that they

have not turned their backs on their people is a good testimony. It will be recalled from the article on church structures that the camp church Christians find functional substitutes for their old religious activities. Add to all this the evidence of lives that have been delivered from alcoholism and immorality; testimonies to healing, peace and joy, and it is not difficult to imagine the level of awareness that this generates.

Another important contribution to evangelism is the bridges that are built through marriage ties. If a man is converted in his wife's camp and becomes a faithful disciple of Christ, he will carry the message to his mother's camp and may be instrumental in starting another church. The camp church then, because it operates <u>within</u> the life-way of the Navajo people, presents them with a living example of Christianity, causing them to consider its implications for their own lives. If they come to the realization that this is the answer to their felt needs then they are ready to talk about making that important decision.

In our American society where the rugged individual has been stressed for so long we forget that other societies put much more emphasis on the group. Whereas we stress the nuclear family (father, mother, and children), most societies stress the extended family or even a larger group. Decisions to put on a religious function, build a house, or to find a wife for one of the boys is thoroughly discussed and consensus is sought before action is taken. With this in mind, let us consider the period of decision in the conversion process.

```
┌─────────────────────────────────────────────┐
│              MISSION COMPOUND                 │
│                                               │
│   Individual Decision                         │
│   Family Resistance                           │
│                      ⬇                        │
├───────────────────────────────────────────────┤
│  P E R I O D    O F    D E C I S I O N        │
├───────────────────────────────────────────────┤
│                      ⬆                        │
│         INDIGENOUS CAMP CHURCH                 │
│                                               │
│   Multi-Individual Decisions                  │
│   Much discussion about merits or demerits    │
│     of Christianity in relation to Navajo     │
│     felt needs. (Alcoholism, Fears, Heal-     │
│     ing, etc.)                                │
└───────────────────────────────────────────────┘
```

The compound church approach to evangelism has placed much emphasis on the individual decision.There is, of course, nothing wrong with this kind of decision; it is the way most of us received Christ.   We admire the convert who stands against the tide and continues to live faithfully for the Lord. The question is, how many do? Letters and records are filled with names of individuals who made such decisions and are no longer following the Lord. It would be well to take note of the instances in Scripture where it tells us that a whole household believed in the Lord. One group working among the Navajos decided about thirty years ago not to baptize the children in their school from non-Christian homes because so few continued in the faith. Many people who have become aware of the implications of the Gospel for their life and have a genuine interest are stumped at this point because they must make a decision contrary to the decision-making processes they have always known. There is resistance from the family because they have not even been consulted. In addition to this, a real opportunity for spreading the good news has been missed.

In the camp church, the indigenous decision-making processes are allowed to operate. There is discussion over the merits and demerits of the Christian way of life. Those who believe they should become

Christians can point out the reasons why. They may
talk about the changes that have come about in the
life of someone who has been converted, or they may
share a testimony they have heard someone give. They
will talk about their felt needs which have not been
satisfied by their own religion. It is at this time
of decision-making that the lives of Christians in
the camp church will be scrutinized. If the fruit of
the Spirit has been evident and the power of God man-
ifested in their lives, there is a strong influence
for a positive decision. This does not mean that
everyone will become a Christian at once; some members
of the family may never become Christians. It may be
that one man or woman may take a step first and over
a period of time others follow. There is no coersion;
if some do not want to follow, their right to their
own choice is respected. It is important to note that
as people align themselves with the indigenous church
they are expected to make a clean break with the old
way. These people know what a model of Christianity
within their own culture means, and they require that
idols be discarded. This is a major step for a Navajo
and one that may be taken with fear and trembling, but
when no ill effects follow, others take note. This is
what Alan Tippett calls "Power Encounter," (1972:126)
akin to the episode of Elijah and the prophets of
Baal on Mount Carmel. This positive step for Christ
is the point of encounter and is the point to which
people will refer when they relate their conversion
experience, although the focus may be on events that
brought them to that point.

The next period is that of incorporation and is
of the utmost importance in the total process of
evangelism. Evangelism does not end with the decision
to accept Christ, but must follow through to incorporation into a local body of believers.

MISSION COMPOUND

Person separates from family and
   lives at mission...
            or
Stays with family as an outsider
   and usually reverts

⬅ no incorporation

P E R I O D   O F   I N C O R P O R A T I O N

⬆

INDIGENOUS CAMP CHURCH

Family church - incorporation automatic
Christian commitment easily observed
Social structure - a reinforcing factor

✓   It is at this very point that our mission compound approach has failed most. Great numbers of
people have made decisions over the years but they
have not continued in the faith. The reason for this,
I believe, was due to the fact that there was no
meaningful group with which they could identify. They
had taken a step which separated them from their family and joined themselves to the missionaries. This
meant that they had to learn a whole new set of signals if they were to communicate. They had to identify with a foreign culture with a different set of
values, some of which were less biblical than their
own. The earnest convert striving to do this might
find life at home more difficult. Since he has joined
himself to the missionary, the family might reason,
"Let the missionary take care of him." The next step
was often a move to the mission where security and
relative comfort might be found. Those who stay at
home without the help or encouragement that the body
of Christ supplies usually revert. This is not to
overlook the faithful few who have clung to their initial commitment to the Lord.

In the camp church incorporation is automatic;
the converts are welcomed with open arms by those who
have been praying for them. There is a definite sense

of belonging, since these are not only brothers and sisters in Christ but blood relatives. The Christian commitment is easily observed for these people live in close contact with one another. There is concern at the first sign of backsliding and much prayer and pressure is brought to bear on the wandering one. So, rather than resistance from the family, there is reinforcement.

Some of the basic felt needs of all humans is to love and be loved, to be recognized and to belong. This is why the Lord of the harvest established the local church, a place where Christians could continue steadfastly in the Apostles' doctrine and in <u>fellowship</u>, in breaking of bread and in prayer. In the Navajo situation, the camp church is effective because it is geographically convenient, culturally relevant and socially satisfying. These churches are small, as are most Navajo churches (35.1 average attendance), but opportunity for wider fellowship is provided at conferences and fellowship meetings, etc.

Alan Tippett adds a fourth period, the Period of Maturity. As he studied areas in the Pacific where there were great losses in the church to nativistic movements, he came to the conclusion that this was most often due to lack of post-baptismal care. There needs to be careful attention given to the "perfecting of the saints." There is the danger of a false prophet, perhaps a disgruntled church leader, who can lead them into some form of neo-paganism. This period of maturity is often initiated by a deep spiritual experience. To some it may be called a new recognition of the Lordship of Christ, to others a Baptism of the Holy Spirit, a Second Blessing, or the Filling of the Spirit. Edwin Orr has said, "A revival can initiate,accelerate or consummate a people movement." It is the point of consummation that we are considering here. The Christian worker should endeavor to provide the means whereby there is opportunity and inspiration for people to make a deep spiritual commitment. There should also be good teaching that will lead people to a consistent devotional life.

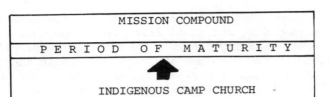

```
┌─────────────────────────────────────────┐
│           MISSION COMPOUND                │
├─────────────────────────────────────────┤
│   P E R I O D   O F   M A T U R I T Y     │
├─────────────────────────────────────────┤
│                  ⬆                        │
│                                           │
│        INDIGENOUS CAMP CHURCH             │
│                                           │
│   Strong Emphasis on Revival              │
│   Much Rededication                       │
│   Opportunity to confess Christ           │
└─────────────────────────────────────────┘
```

In the camp churches we have observed, there is a lot of opportunity to rededicate one's life to the Lord. Some of them have many "revival" meetings where Christians are admonished to renew their commitment. There is usually a prolonged period for testimonies which not only strengthens the speaker but encourages the listeners.

Some of these camp churches have able and knowledgeable pastors, others have pastors with very little training. It is at this point that I see the greatest weakness in many of these churches. There is real need for some kind of training for these men if the churches are to grow in grace and avoid the pitfalls of false doctrine or even reversion to the old religion.

CONCLUSION

As mentioned earlier, these two examples are at opposite poles and many churches have elements of both approaches. We must be willing to ask ourselves if the methods or programs we are pursuing are moving people from the non-Christian to the Christian context. In other words, are there responsible Christians and responsible, reproducing congregations. The camp church is reproducable by Navajos; the compound church is not.

If we are working with churches in the developing communities where people are not living in the traditional social structure, we should at least be aware of their felt needs and adjust our ministry accordingly. To transport a model or program from South Bend, Indiana, or Houston, Texas, is the height of irrelevance.

NOTES

1. As told to the authors by Herman Williams, Navajo Mountain Pastor.

2. Donald McGavran defines a people movement as a multi-individual, mutually interdependant conversion. It is a process whereby a homogeneous group, tribe or society decides to become Christians. It is multi-individual because each person makes a personal decision, but this is done after much consideration and discussion as a group. It is hard for individualistic Euroamericans to grasp this process, yet McGavran points out that two-thirds to three-fourths of peoples in Asia, Latin America and Africa who have become Christians have come in precisely this manner (1970:302).

3. See Church Structures of the Black Mesa Church

8

The Navajos Today:
Resistant or Receptive?

A current myth among missionaries is that the Navajos are a resistant people. On the contrary, never before have the Navajos been so receptive.[1] Never before have there been so many Navajo pastors, such a well trained work force, so rapid a multiplication of churches. Never before have there been so many indigenous churches, or have Navajo Christians built their own church buildings and paid their own pastors. Never before have so many of the people heard the Gospel, never have so many young adults known the facts of the Gospel. Never before have there been television sets in Navajo homes broadcasting religious programs, never such rapid acculturation, and never before have so many churches run over 100 in attendance. Never before has there been the cooperation that exists among the missionaries on the Reservation. Never before has there been such a need for an aggressive program of evangelism and church planting.

How many Navajo people are unevangelized and how near is the field to harvest? While the growth is comforting, there is still much to be done. How will the remaining 142,605 people be evangelized? What is the process of evangelization and how ripe is the field?

James Engel (1975:45) has given us an evangelism countdown that has been used by many at the School of World Mission and has gone through several adaptations. We have taken the liberty of adapting it even farther. (C. Peter Wagner uses the terms "presence," "proclamation" and "persuasion" evangelism and we

have added the definitions for each.)   It is a valuable tool.   It is helpful to give us a visible picture of where the Navajos started and how far they
have moved toward being a field that is ripe to harvest since the first missionaries began working among
them.

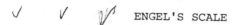 ENGEL'S SCALE

Presence Evangelism moves people from non-acceptance to acceptance of the communicator	-10 awareness of a Su-preme Being - 9 no effective knowl-edge of Christian-ity - 8 initial awareness of Christianity - 7 interest and accep-tance of communica-tor
Proclamation Evangelism moves people from non-acceptance to acceptance of the Gospel	- 6 awareness of the fundamentals of the Gospel - 5 grasp of implica-tions - 4 positive attitude - 3 personal problem
Persuasion Evangelism moves people from non-acceptance to	- 2 challenge to deci-sion - 1 repentance
A NEW DISCIPLE BORN (Matt. 28:19,20)	
acceptance of being a disciple of Jesus and a faithful mem-ber of His church	+ 1 reflection and in-corporation + 2 obedience-oriented Christian (Matt.28: 19,20) + 3 reproducing Chris-tian

    To show graphically what has happened and what
the present status of Christianity is on the Navajo
Reservation, we use the Engle scale covering four
periods of time.

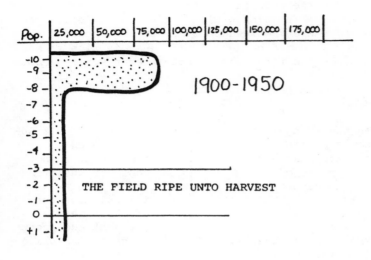

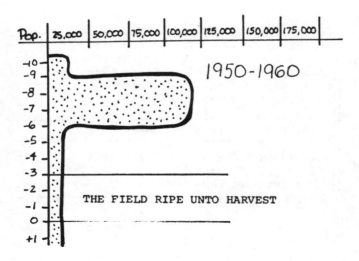

The Receptivity of the Navajo People to Christianity
in Four Different Periods of Time on the Engels Scale

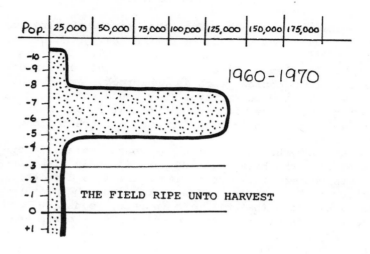

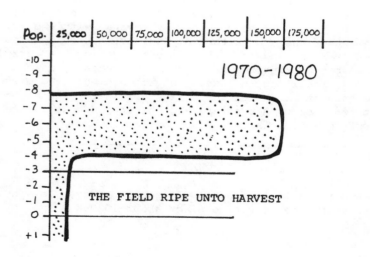

The Receptivity of the Navajo People to Christianity
in Four Different Periods of Time on the Engels Scale

REAPING THE HARVEST

Mission churches with the right mixture are growing in both rural areas like Navajo Mountain, Inscription House, Leupp, Naschitti, Tohlakai, Newcomb, Toadlena, Dennehotso, and Pinon, and in developing communities such as Shiprock, Crownpoint, Ft. Defiance and Tuba City. They could and should be growing everywhere with the right mixture of ingredients and the right program for each different homogeneous unit.

However,they will not be harvested unless laborers go into the harvest and persuade this ripe harvest to become disciples of Jesus Christ and faithful members of His Church. The church must be prepared with a program that will incorporate, conserve and send forth these converts. Missionaries who are anxious for a harvest should be asking every new convert, "Who do you know that is talking about becoming a Christian, or even thinking about it?" An endless stream of converts can be found through this method.

Missionaries should look for a harvest within the next ten years. All missionaries and Navajo Christians should be praying for revival within every segment of the church that now exists. Missionaries must look up and see the harvest ripening and pray for laborers that the harvest may be reaped and conserved, resulting in lasting church growth. To miss the harvest and see the grain fall in the field and rot for lack of harvesters and church planters is the worst form of unfaithfulness to God.

NOTES

1. According to the Scates-Dolaghan Survey, Navajos have become receptive since about 1960.

BIBLIOGRAPHY

ENGEL, JAMES F. and WILBERT H. NORTON.
    1975 What's Gone Wrong With the Harvest?
          Eerdmans, Grand Rapids.

Receiving the New Translation of Navajo Scripture.

Tent Revival, Navajo Reading Class, Gateway, Colorado.

The Crystal Choir Sings.

Red Mesa Full Gospel Church
(Jack Nakai, pastor), Red Mesa, Arizona.

St. Christopher's Episcopal Church - Bluff.

Assembly of God, Ft. Defiance.

Cactus Valley NGM Camp Church.

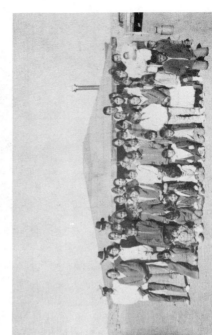

Elsie Begaz Teaching Children at Pinon Church

Congregation at Middle Mesa Baptist Church
(June 1970, Pastor John Mexicano)

Fannie Scott –
Navajo Woman Teaching Literary Class

Red Mesa Camp Church (Pastor Jim Charley)

A Survey of
Navajo Churches

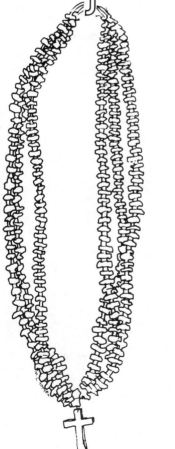

DENOMINATIONS	CHURCHES	PEOPLE ATTENDING	NAVAJO PASTORS	ANGLO PASTORS	AVERAGE SIZE CHURCH	LARGEST CHURCH
Assembly of God	32	1,699	9	20	58.6	200
Baptist	62	2,545	32	24	41	160
GARB						
Conservative						
Southern						
Independent						
American (1)						
Brethren	6	245	4	2	41	70
Dunkard (1)						
Grace (2)						
Church of Brethren (1)						
Brethren in Christ (2)						
Christian Churches (Independent)	6	148	5	1	29	50
Christian Reformed	20	1,270	13	8	57.7	220
Church of Christ	7	213	1	7	30	48
Christian Missionary Alliance	1	100	3	0	100	100
Episcopal	10	282	1	4	31	85
Friends	3	80	2	2	27	40
Lutheran Evangelical	3	95	2	3	32	40

DENOMINATIONS	CHURCHES	PEOPLE ATTENDING	NAVAJO PASTORS	ANGLO PASTORS	AVERAGE SIZE CHURCH	LARGEST CHURCH
Mennonite						
Church of God in Christ						
Black Mountain	6	145	3	3	29	50
Methodist						
United	3	110	2	1	55	60
Wesleyan	6	110	1	4	22	40
Free	2					
Nazarene	17	775	12	4	45.6	80
Pentecostal	76	2,153	73	0	28.1	100
(Indigenous)						
Full-Gospel						
Church of God						
Word of God						
Pentecostal	24	725	2	19	30.2	80
Holiness						
United						
Independent						
Church of God						
Presbyterian	11	365	4	3	33.1	150
Non-denominational	44	1,435	31	15	34.2	100
Seventh Day Adventist	4					
TOTALS	343	12,395	203	121	35.1	

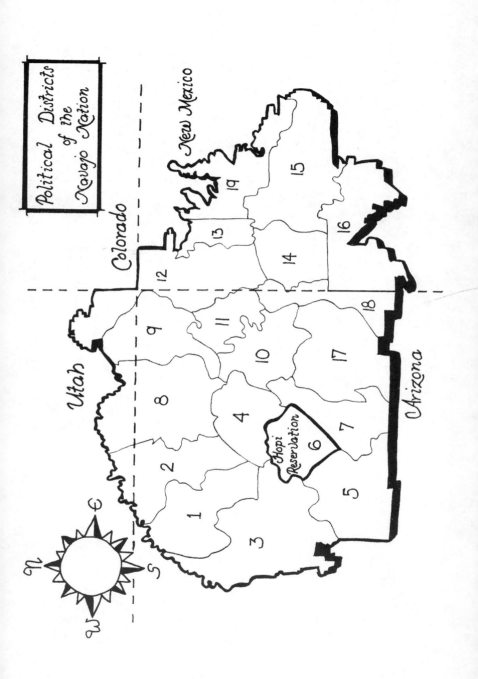

Political Districts of the Navajo Nation

District 1

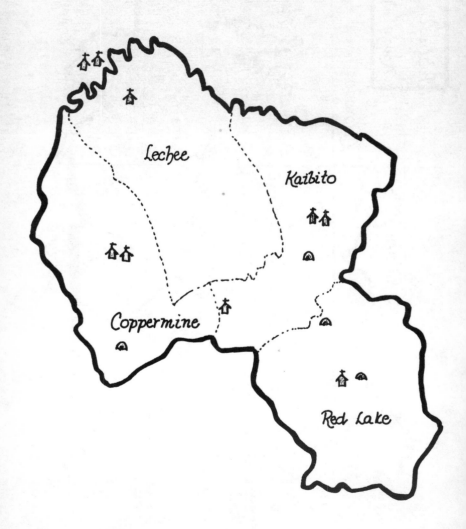

Lechee

Kaibito

Coppermine

Red Lake

District 1
Church Statistics

♟ 9 Mission churches
♣ 4 Camp churches
380 Average Navajo weekly attendance
5,152 Navajo population
7.4% Protestant church attendance

Red Lake
   White Mesa Baptist House Church
   Full-Gospel
   Grace Brethren

Kaibito
   Presbyterian
   Nazarene
   Full-Gospel
   Baptist

Lechee
   Nazarene

Coppermine
   Middle Mesa Baptist
   Coppermine Baptist
   Full-Gospel

Page
   Nazarene
   Baptist

District 2

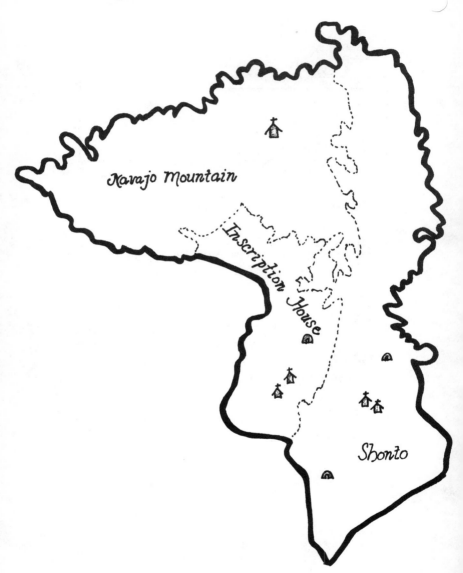

Navajo Mountain

Inscription House

Shonto

District 2
Church Statistics

♠ 5 Mission churches
♠ 3 Camp churches
470 Average Navajo weekly attendance
4,018 Navajo population
11.6% Protestant church attendance

Inscription House
  Inscription House Navajo Mission
  Red Mesa Baptist
  Full-Gospel

Shonto
  Black Mesa Baptist House Church
  Assembly of God
  Christian Catholic
  Full-Gospel

Navajo Mountain
  Christian Missionary Alliance

District 3

Bodaway

Tuba City

Cameron

Coalmine Mesa

District 3
Church Statistics

⛪ 15 Mission churches
🛖 2 Camp churches
455 Average Navajo weekly attendance
6,426 Navajo population
7.1% Protestant church attendance

Bodaway
    Hidden Springs Flagstaff Mission to the
        Navajos
    Cedar Ridge Baptist
    Gap Assembly of God
    Gap Flagstaff Mission to the Navajos

Tuba City
    Church of Christ
    Presbyterian
    Baptist (3)
    Assembly of God
    Full-Gospel

Coalmine Mesa
    Baptist
    Black Falls Flagstaff Mission to the
        Navajos

Cameron
    Baptist
    Assembly of God
    Full-Gospel
    Flagstaff Mission to the Navajos

District 4

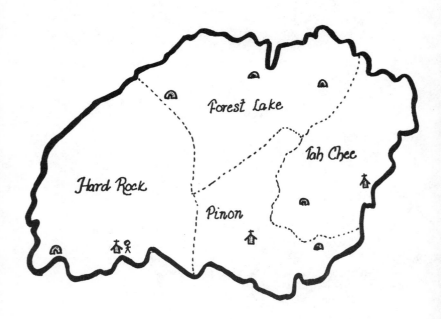

Forest Lake

Tah Chee

Hard Rock

Pinon

District 4
Church Statistics

```
♟ 3     Mission churches
♠ 6     Camp churches
♀ 1     School
266     Average Navajo weekly attendance
9,700   Navajo population
2.7%    Protestant church attendance
```

Hard Rock
    Navajo Gospel Mission
    Full-Gospel

Forest Lake
    Forest Lake House Church
    Oak Ridge Friends
    Cactus Valley House Church

Pinon
    Navajo Gospel Mission Church
    Whippoorwill House Church

Tah Chee
    Burnt Corn House Church
    Mennonite

District 5

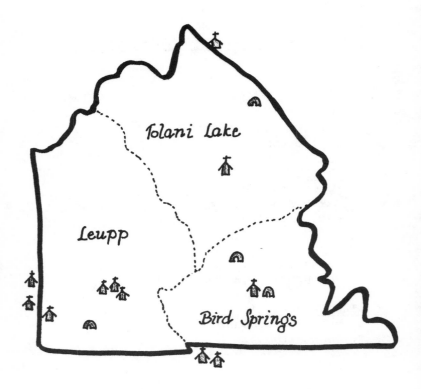

Tolani Lake

Leupp

Bird Springs

District 5
Church Statistics

🏠 11 Mission churches
⛺ 4 Camp churches
500 Average Navajo weekly attendance
3,749 Navajo population
13.3% Protestant church attendance

Leupp
    Grand Falls Flagstaff Mission to the
        Navajos
    Presbyterian
    Leupp Nazarene
    Round Cedar Nazarene
    Baptist
    Canyon Diablo Baptist House Church
    Navajo Trails Tabernacle

Tolani Lake
    Tonalea Pentecostal Church of God
    Sand Springs Navajo Gospel Mission
        Church
    Camp Church

Bird Springs
    Baptist
    Baptist Camp Church
    Ninety and Nine Indian Mission
    Full-Gospel
    Navajo Christian Church

Note: There is no District 6.

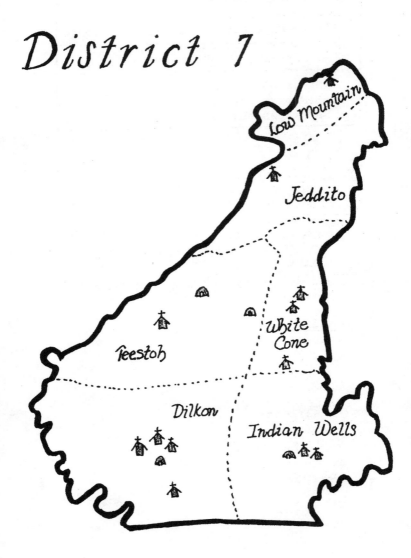

District 7

```
♟ 12 Mission churches
 ♠ 4 Camp churches
 571 Average Navajo weekly attendance
7,532 Navajo population
7.6% Protestant church attendance
```

Low Mountain
  Smoke Signal Nazarene

Jeddito
  Keams Baptist

White Cone
  Baptist (2)
  Assembly of God

Teestoh
  Fingerpoint Navajo Gospel Mission
    Church
  Assembly of God
  Baptist House Church

Indian Wells
  Presbyterian
  Assembly of God
  Sunflower Butte Full-Gospel

Dilkon
  Christian Church
  Nazarene
  Montezuma Chair Nazarene
  Castle Butte Pentecostal Navajo Indian
    Mission
  Castle Butte Full-Gospel

District 8

Oljato

Kayenta

Dennehotso

Chilchinbito

District 8
Church Statistics

🔔 10 Mission churches
🔔 3 Camp churches
531 Average Navajo weekly attendance
7,378 Navajo population
7.2% Protestant church attendance

Oljato
  Episcopal
  Presbyterian
  Full-Gospel
  S.D.A. Church

Kayenta
  Flagstaff Mission to the Navajos
  Church of Christ
  Presbyterian
  Assembly of God
  Pentecostal Church of God

Dennehotso
  Presbyterian
  Assembly of God

Chilchinbito
  White Grass House Church
  Coal Mine House Church
  Nazarene

District 9

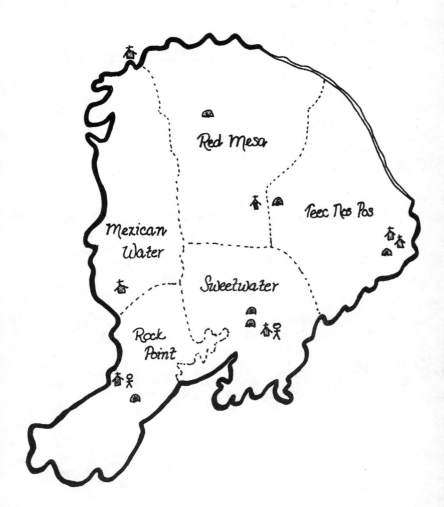

Red Mesa

Teec Nos Pos

Mexican
Water

Sweetwater

Rock
Point

District 9
Church Statistics

```
 🏠  7    Mission churches
 ⛺  6    Camp churches
 👤  2    Schools
    403    Average Navajo weekly attendance
  7,177    Navajo population
    5.6%   Protestant church attendance
```

Red Mesa
  Full-Gospel
  Christian Church

Mexican Water
  Baptist
  Bluff Episcopal

Teec Nos Pos
  Christian Reformed
  Baptist
  Full-Gospel
  Christian House Church

Sweetwater
  Emmanuel Mission
  Christian Church
  Full-Gospel

Rock Point
  Lutheran
  Full-Gospel

District 10

13 Mission churches
2 Camp churches
2 Schools
526 Average Navajo weekly attendance
10,853 Navajo population
4.8% Protestant church attendance

Rough Rock
    Friends Mission

Many Farms
    Lutheran
    Church of Christ
    Baptist
    Pentecostal House Church

Chinle
    Del Muerto Presbyterian
    Chinle Presbyterian
    Del Muerto Baptist
    Chinle Baptist
    Full-Gospel
    S.D.A. Church

Tselani
    Mennonite - Black Mountain
    Mennonite - Tsalina
    Cottonwood Full-Gospel

Nazalini
    Presbyterian

District 11

Round Rock

Lukachukai

Tsailee—Wheatfields

District 11
Church Statistics

```
   1 Mission church
   3 Camp churches
   1 School
  80 Average Navajo weekly attendance
3,974 Navajo population
  2% Protestant church attendance
```

Round Rock
    Baptist

Lukachukai
    Full-Gospel (2)

Tsailee-Wheatfields
    Baptist House Church

District 12

District 12 continued
Church Statistics

Aneth

🛕	20 Mission churches
⛺	13 Camp churches
	1,355 Average Navajo weekly attendance
	18,439 Navajo population
	7.2% Protestant church attendance

Shiprock

Beclahbito

Shiprock

Red Rock

Sanostee

Two Grey Hills

Sheep Springs

Aneth
Montezuma Creek Navajo Gospel Crusade
Aneth Navajo Gospel Crusade
Montezuma Creek Episcopal
Montezuma Creek Church of Christ
Full-Gospel

Shiprock
Christian Reformed
Full-Gospel (3)
Episcopal
Church of Christ
Methodist
Baptist (2)
Assembly of God

Beclahbito
Baptist
Full-Gospel
Christian Church
Christian Reformed

Sanostee
Christian Reformed
Free Methodist
Full-Gospel (2)

Red Rock
Christian Reformed
Cove Assembly of God
Full-Gospel
Oak Springs Full-Gospel
New Testament Full-Gospel Church

Two Grey Hills
Toadalena Christian Reformed
Newcomb Christian Reformed
Assembly of God
United Pentecostal

Sheep Springs
Full-Gospel

District 13

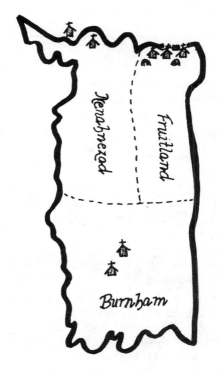

District 13
Church Statistics

🔔 7 Mission churches
🏕 2 Camp churches
308 Average Navajo weekly attendance
3,815 Navajo population
8% Protestant church attendance

Nenahnezad
    Assembly of God
    Hogback Church of Christ

Fruitland
    Episcopal
    Baptist
    Assembly of God
    Waterflow Pentecostal Church
    Indian Holiness-Wesleyan

Burnham
    Christian Reformed
    Baptist

District 14

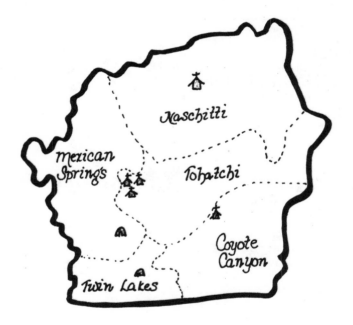

Naschitti

Mexican
Springs

Tohatchi

Coyote
Canyon

Twin Lakes

District 14
Church Statistics

```
🏛 5 Mission churches
🏕 2 Camp churches
   320 Average Navajo weekly attendance
7,590 Navajo population
  4.3% Protestant church attendance
```

Naschitti
    Christian Reformed

Tohatchi
    Christian Reformed
    Baptist
    United Pentecostal

Mexican Springs
    Full-Gospel

Coyote Canyon
    Baptist

Twin Lakes
    Full-Gospel

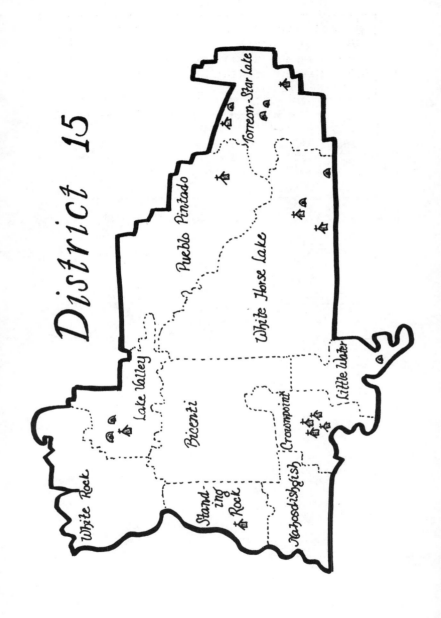

District 15

♣ 12 Mission churches
♠ 8 Camp churches
695 Average Navajo weekly attendance
8,520 Navajo population
8% Protestant church attendance

Pueblo Pintado
    Assembly of God

Torreon-Star Lake
    Star Lake Bible Mission
    Torreon Navajo Brethren, Dunkard
    Tinian Full-Gospel
    Full-Gospel
    Star Lake Lighthouse Mission

Standing Rock
    Baptist

Little Water
    Borrego Pass Full-Gospel

Lake Valley
    Chaco Canyon Brethren in Christ
    Full-Gospel (2)
    S.D.A. Church

Crownpoint
    Christian Reformed
    Baptist (2)
    Assembly of God

White Horse Lake
    Christian Reformed
    Free Methodist
    Full-Gospel (2)

District 16

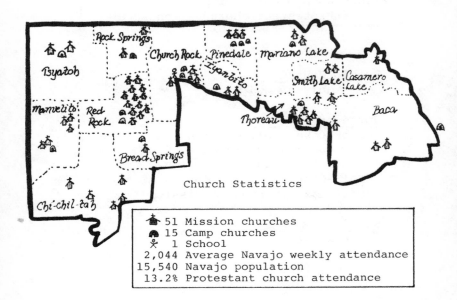

Church Statistics

```
🏛 51    Mission churches
🏕 15    Camp churches
🎒  1    School
2,044    Average Navajo weekly attendance
15,540   Navajo population
13.2%    Protestant church attendance
```

Tsayatoh
    Black Hat Assembly of God
    Black Hat Mission
    Black Hat Oral Roberts Church

Rock Springs
    Tolahkai Christian Reformed
    Gospel Truth Mission
    Phillip Cove House Church

Pinedale
    Christian Reformed
    Baptist
    Assembly of God
    Holiness Indian Mission
    Church of God
    Full-Gospel

Church Rock
    Elim Haven Mission
    Christian Reformed
    Rehobeth Christian Reformed
    Full-Gospel
    Kit Carson Cave Church of God (2)

Mariano Lake
    Berean Mission
    Friends
    Full-Gospel

Smith Lake
    Mt. Powell Baptist
    Lake Powell Jct. Baptist
    Smith Lake Baptist
    Pentecostal

Bread Springs
    Pine Haven Baptist
    Church of God

Chi-chil-tah
    Pinetree Mission
    Jones Ranch Baptist
    Baptist
    Whitewater Gospel Mission
    United Indian Mission Camp

Red Rock
    Mentmore Mission
    Gallup Christian Reformed
    Tolahkai Christian Reformed
    Baptist
    Assembly of God
    Church of God
    All Nations Mission
    Independent Pentecostal
    Pentecostal Church of God
    Four-Square
    United Pentecostal
    Rocky Point Church of God
    Free Trinity Navajo Mission
    Full-Gospel
    Bible Baptist Shepherd

Manuelito
    Bible School and Mission - Defiance
    Bible School and Mission - Manuelito
    Twin Butte Nazarene
    Defiance Pentecostal Church
    Full-Gospel
    Pentecostal Church of God

Iyanbito
    Wingate Christian Reformed
    Wingate Baptist
    Perea Pentecostal Church
        of God

Baca
    Prewitt Wesleyan
    Prewitt Assembly of God
    Haystack Full-Gospel
    Christian Reformed

Thoreau
    Berean
    Crossland Mission
    Baptist
    Thoreau Revival Center
    Church of God

Casamero Lake
    Church of Christ

District 17

Steamboat

Ganado

Kinlichee

Cornfields

Klagetoh

Greasewood

Wide Ruins

District 17
Church Statistics

```
🔔 10 Mission churches
🛖  8 Camp churches
   580 Average Navajo weekly attendance
10,310 Navajo population
 5.6% Protestant church attendance
```

Steamboat
  Baptist
  Toyei Full-Gospel
  Full-Gospel

Cornfields
  Assembly of God
  Presbyterian

Ganado
  Alcoholic Rehabilitation Center
  Presbyterian
  Baptist
  Full-Gospel
  Baptist Family Church

Klagetoh-Wide Ruins
  Mennonite (2)
  Pentecostal Church of God
  Chambers Wesleyan Holiness

Greasewood
  Mennonite
  Navajo Station Nazarene
  Full-Gospel
  Pentecostal Holiness

District 18

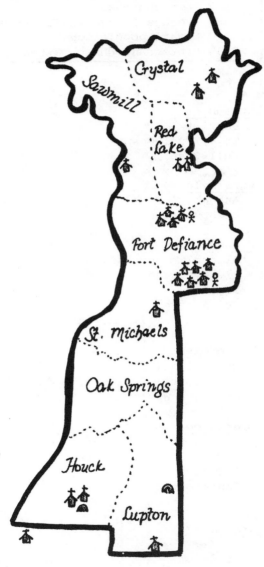

Sawmill

Crystal

Red Lake

Fort Defiance

St. Michaels

Oak Springs

Houck

Lupton

District 18
Church Statistics

⌂ 20 Mission churches
🏠 2 Camp churches
🧍 2 Schools
808 Average Navajo weekly attendance
11,127 Navajo population
7.3% Protestant church attendance

Crystal
  Navajo Bible School and Mission
  Baptist

Sawmill
  Episcopal

Red Lake
  Navajo Lutheran
  Episcopal

Ft. Defiance
  Navajo Bible School and Mission
  Bible Church
  Christian Reformed
  Episcopal
  Church of Christ
  Methodist
  Nazarene
  Assembly of God
  Baptist
  Mennonite Hogan Hozhoni

Lupton
  Andersontown Mission
  Full-Gospel

St. Michaels
  Navajo Evangelical Mission

Houck
  Good News Mission
  Sanders Bible Mission
  Assembly of God
  Church of God

District 19

Huerfano

Kageezi

Counselors

Ojo Encino

District 19
Church Statistics

🔔 10 Mission churches
🔔 5 Camp churches
566 Average Navajo weekly attendance
6,281 Navajo population
9% Protestant church attendance

Huerfano
    Berean Mission
    Miracle Full-Gospel
    Carson Episcopal
    Bisti Methodist
    Carson Assembly of God
    Twin Pines Full-Gospel
    Gallegos Full-Gospel
    Bisti Pentecostal House Church
    Bloomfield Brethren in Christ

Nageezi
    Kinebito Baptist
    Full-Gospel
    Lybrook Church of the Brethren

Ojo Encino
    Assembly of God

Counsellors
    Brethren
    Pine Hill Baptist

Note: There is no District 20.

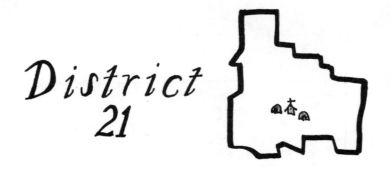

District
21

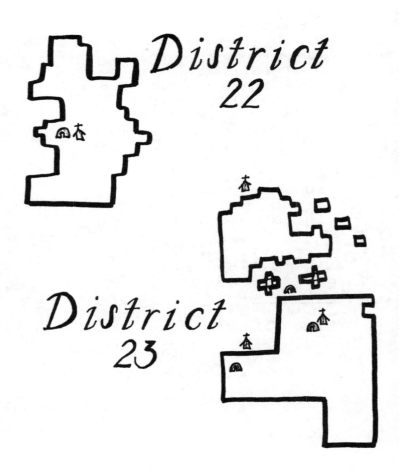

District
22

District
23

District 21
Church Statistics

```
 1 Mission church
 2 Camp churches
80 Average Navajo weekly attendance
1,303 Navajo population
6% Protestant church attendance
```

Canoncito
Full-Gospel Pentecostal House Church
Full-Gospel Word of God Church
Baptist

District 22
Church Statistics

```
 1 Mission church
 1 Camp church
85 Average Navajo weekly attendance
1,060 Navajo population
8% Protestant church attendance
```

Alamo
Baptist
Full-Gospel Word of God Church

District 23
Church Statistics

```
 3 Mission churches
 3 Camp churches
200 Average Navajo weekly attendance
1,604 Navajo population
12.5% Protestant church attendance
```

Ramah
Nazarene (3)
Pentecostal Church of God (2)
Neesjia Baptist Church of God

135

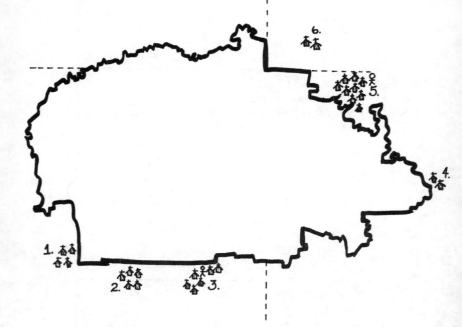

Border Towns

Border Towns
Church Statistics

1-Flagstaff, Arizona
Flagstaff Mission to the Navajos
American Indian Mission
Baptist
Assembly of God

2-Winslow, Arizona
Nazarene
Baptist (2)
Assembly of God
Pentecostal Church of God

3-Holbrook, Arizona
Seventh-Day Adventist School
Baptist
Assembly of God
Harvest Time Mission
Twin Wells School
John 3:16 Mission
S.D.A. Church

4-Cuba, New Mexico
Baptist
Methodist

5-Farmington, New Mexico
American Indian Bible Mission
Navajo Bible Mission
Christian Reformed (2)
Episcopal
Baptist
Assembly of God
Desert View Mission
Church of God
Farmington Methodist Mission School

6-Cortez, Colorado
Christian Revival Fellowship
Navajo Gospel Crusade

A Directory of Pastors and Churches

Directories are constantly dated and this one is no exception. People are on the move and new churches and pastors are added month by month.

For this reason and the fact that we know there will be errors, we hesitated to include this directory. However, it is an important part of a survey such as this and we must begin somewhere. So we are asking for your understanding and help. If there are any corrections or additions please send them to Tom Dolaghan, P. O. Box 446, Pinon, AZ 86510. We will publish a new directory with fewer errors and not quite so dated.

A Directory of Pastors and Churches

ASSEMBLY OF GOD

Assembly of God Mission
    Steven Brown
    311 E. Erie, Box 91, Holbrook, AZ 86025
Broken Arrow Chapel
    Elsie Watson
    Indian Wells, AZ 86031
Calvary Assembly of God (Black Hat)
    Mary Buttonbuck
    Window Rock, AZ 86515
Carson Assembly of God
    Elmer Brown
    Carson, NM 87517
Cornfield Assembly of God
    Rev. Musgrove
    Ganado, AZ 86505
Cove Assembly of God
    Willie John Willie
    Shiprock, NM 87420
Dennehotso Assembly of God
    Kayenta, AZ 86033
Ft. Defiance Assembly of God
    Duane Johnson/Luke Yazzie
    Box 92, Ft. Defiance, AZ 86504
Gallup Indian Assembly of God
    Roy Nelson
    Box 1780, Gallup, NM 86301
Gap Assembly of God
    Tuba City, AZ 86045
Independent Assembly of God
    John Billy
    Fruitland, NM 87416
Indian Assembly of God
    Margaret Slane
    1729 N. Main, Flagstaff, AZ 86001

Indian Assembly of God
   Lyle Wolverton
   617 Alfred, Winslow, AZ 86047
Kayenta Assembly of God
   A.C. Tyson
   Kayenta, AZ 86033
Mesa View Assembly of God
   Charley Lee
   Shiprock, NM 87420
Navajo Assembly of God
   Evan Campbell
   2121 Camino Rio, Farmington, NM 87401
Navajo Assembly of God
   Allen Goetjen
   Box 165, Houck, AZ 86506
Navajo Trails Assembly of God
   Valda Brown
   Box 64, Cameron, AZ 86020
Nena Nazad Navajo Assembly of God
   James Yellowman
   Farmington, NM 87401
Newcomb Assembly of God
   Tohatchi, NM 87325
Ojo Encino Assembly of God
   Rev. Bruten
   Box 673, Cuba, NM 87013
Pentecostal Assembly of God
   Leonard Everly
   Crownpoint, NM 87313
Pinedale Assembly of God
   Luis B. Yazzie
   Church Rock, NM 87311
Prewitt Assembly of God Indian Mission
   Jim Reeves
   Prewitt, NM 87045
Pueblo Pintado Assembly of God
   Marvin Martin
   Crownpoint, NM 87313
Shonto Assembly of God
   Ken Delaney
   Box 885, Kayenta, AZ 86033

Teastoh Assembly of God
     Paul Hodson
     Star Route, Winslow, AZ 86047
Tuba City Assembly of God
     James Horne
     Box 948, Tuba City, AZ 86045
White Cone Assembly of God
     Roberta Roanhorse
     Indian Wells, AZ 86031

                    BAPTIST

AMERICAN
American Baptist Mission
     Arthur L. Sanford
     Box 67, Keams Canyon, AZ 86034

CONSERVATIVE
Black Mesa Camp Church
     Dick Begay
     Tonalea, AZ 86044
Cedar Ridge Baptist Church
     Harry Sloan
     Tuba City, AZ 86045
Coalmine Baptist Church
     Kii Littleman
     Oraibi, AZ 86039
Coppermine Church
     Lee Begay
     Box 31, Tuba City, AZ 86045
First Navajo Baptist
     Jerry Sloan
     Box 1198, Tuba City, AZ 86045
Middle Mesa Baptist Church
     John Mexicano
     Box 254, Tuba City, AZ 86045
Porcupine Ridge Church
     Jimmy Mexicano
     Tuba City, AZ 86045

Red Mesa Baptist Church
   Alex Morez
   Tonalea, AZ 86044
Tse Bi Ootseel Baptist Church (White Cone)
   Lemuel Yazzie
   Box Y, Indian Wells, AZ 86031

G.A.R.B.
Berean Baptist Mission
   DeWitt Pritchard
   Box 731, Holbrook, AZ 86025
Bird Springs Baptist Church
   Art Woodard
   Box 908, Winslow, AZ 86047
Cedar Baptist Church
   Rev. Gaston
   Jones Ranch, Gallup, NM 86301
Indian Baptist
   Winslow, AZ 86047
Mexican Water Baptist
   Duane Block/David Gilwood
   R-1, Box 2F, Cortez, CO 81321
Rainbow Baptist Mission
   Jimmy Draper/Bill Anderson
   Box 565, Chinle, AZ 86503

INDEPENDENT
Bethel Navajo Baptist Church
   Harold Noble
   Steamboat, Ganado, AZ 86505
Bible Baptist Church
   Pat Natoni
   Ganado, AZ 86505
Bible Baptist Shepherd Mission
   Don Corley
   1105 S. Miller, Farmington, NM 87401
Bible Baptist Shepherd Mission
   Edward Hannig
   507 N. 5th Street, Gallup, NM 86301
Bird Springs Camp Church
   Henry Kii Yazzie
   Star Route, Winslow, AZ 86047

Burnham Baptist Church
    Roger Deal
    P.O. Box 292, Fruitland, NM 87416
Canyon Diablo Baptist Church
    Harry Russell
    Rt. 1, Box 43, Flagstaff, AZ 86001
Dok View Baptist Church
    Jimmy Seaton
    Chilchilto, Vander Wagon, NM 87326
Faith Navajo Baptist
    John Bacora
    Thoreau, NM 87323
First Navajo Baptist
    Jimmy A. Ettsitty
    Box 308, Crownpoint, NM 87313
        ...Coyote Canyon Baptist
        ...Smith Lake Baptist
        ...Lake Powell Baptist
Fruitland Baptist Church
    Roger Deal
    P.O. Box 292, Fruitland, NM 87416
Ganado Baptist Church
    Rev. Godoby
    Ganado, AZ 86505
Memorial Baptist Church
    Lee Pearson
    Box 522, Chinle, AZ 86503
Mount Powell Mission
    Frank Booker
    Box 665, Thoreau, NM 87323
Pine Haven Navajo Baptist Church
    Charles Girton
    Box 686, Gallup, NM 87301
Round Rock Baptist Church
    Elliott Hogue
    Round Rock Trading Post, Chinle, AZ 86503
Shiprock Baptist Temple
    Rev. Walker
    Shiprock, NM 87420
    (meets in the DNA building)

SOUTHERN
Alamo Indian Baptist
    Dennis Apachita
    Box 722, Magdalena, NM 87825
Beclabito Indian Baptist Church
    Vernon Barton
    Box 907, Shiprock, NM 87420
Cameron Indian Baptist Church
    Jasper Jones
    3221 Elder Drive, Flagstaff, AZ 86001
Canoncito Indian Baptist
    Wallace Castillo
    Box 444, Canoncito, NM 87026
Church Rock Indian Baptist Church
    Keith Begay
    Box 15, Church Rock, NM 87311
Crownpoint Indian Baptist Church
    Austin Toledo
    Box 176, Crownpoint, NM 87313
Dry Lake Indian Baptist Church
    Lemuel Littleman
    43 Brannen Homes, Flagstaff, AZ 86001
Farmington Indian Baptist
    Irene Diswood
    Box 1892, Farmington, NM 87401
First Indian Baptist
    W. C. Buie
    501 S. 3rd, Gallup, NM 86301
First Southern Baptist
    Wade H. Robertson
    Box 448, Window Rock, AZ 86515
First Indian Baptist
    Allison Holman
    905 W. Aspenwall, Winslow, AZ 86047
        ...White Cone: Holman/Jack Begay
Ft. Wingate Indian Baptist
    Ft. Wingate, NM 87316
Indian Baptist
    Kenneth Norton
    Box 233, Fruitland, NM 87416

Indian Baptist
   A. A. Moore
   Box 1794, Flagstaff, AZ 86001
Kimbeto Indian Baptist
   David McKenzie
   Nageezi, NM 87037
Leupp Indian Baptist
   William Parham
   Box 848, Winslow, AZ 86047
Many Farms Indian Baptist
   Calvin Sandlin
   Box 8, Chinle, AZ 86503
Navajo Trails Baptist
   Box 215, Tuba City, AZ 86045
Ojoencino Indian Baptist
   Cuba, NM 87013
Pine Hill Indian Baptist
   Box 44, Counselor, NM 87018
Ramah Indian Baptist
   Ollie Blevins
   Box 2905, Grants, NM 87020
Shiprock Indian Baptist Church
   George Nez
   Box 907, Shiprock, NM 87420
Standing Rock Bible Baptist Shepherd
   Neil Foerster
   Box 1257, Crownpoint, NM 87313
Teec Nos Pos Indian Baptist Church
   Tom Nelson
   Box 916, Teec Nos Pos, AZ 86514
Tinian Indian Baptist Church
   Cecil Willeto
   Box 84, Counselor, NM 87018
Tohatchi Indian Baptist Church
   Paul Kloffer
   Box 267, Tohatchi, NM 87325
White Horse Indian Baptist Church
   Crownpoint, NM 87313

BRETHREN

Brethren in Christ
   Cicil Werito/Marion Heisey
   Chaco Canyon National Monument
   Bloomfield, NM 87413
Brethren in Christ
   John Peter Yazzie
   Blanco Trading Post, Bloomfield, NM 87413
Community Navajo Grace Brethren Church
   John Trujillo
   Counselor, NM 87018
Grace Brethren
   Nelson Betoni
   Box 17, Tonalea, AZ 86044
Lybrook Community Ministries, Church of the
   Brethren
   Russell Kiester
   Star Route 4, Cuba, NM 87013
Torreon Navajo Brethren Mission (Dunkard)
   David Sciler
   Box 188, Cuba, NM 87013

CHRISTIAN CHURCH

Dilcon Christian Church
   Ernest Creamer/Raymond Joey
   Star Route, Winslow, AZ 86047
Navajo Christian Churches
   David Scates, Vernon Hollett, Jim Charley,
      Directors
   Box 1049, Teec Nos Pos, AZ 86514
   ...Red Mesa - Jim Charley/Larry Johnson
   ...Sweetwater - Alfred Nargo
   ...Beclahbito - Harvey Yazzie
   ...Borrego Pass - Kee Tapaha
   ...Cudei - Lloyd Harrison

CHRISTIAN MISSIONARY ALLIANCE

Navajo Mountain Mission
    Herman Williams
    Navajo Mountain, Tonalea, AZ 86044
Piute Canyon Camp Church
    Pete Greyeyes
    Navajo Mountain Mission, Tonalea, AZ 86044

CHRISTIAN REFORMED

Burnham Christian Reformed
    Sampson Yazzie
    618 W. Arrington Street, Farmington, NM 87401
Church Rock Christian Reformed
    Tony Begay
    Box 45, Church Rock, NM 87311
Crownpoint Christian Reformed
    Gordon Stuit/Howard Begay
    Box 208, Crownpoint, NM 87313
Farmington Christian Reformed
    Sampson Yazzie
    618 W. Arrington Street, Farmington, NM 87401
Fort Wingate Christian Reformed
    Gerrit T. Haagsma
    Box 388, Fort Wingate, NM 87316
Gallup Christian Reformed
    Alfred Mulder
    1225 Country Club Dr., Gallup, NM 87301
Naschitti Christian Reformed
    Corwin Brummel
    Naschitti, NM 87325
Navajo Christian Reformed
    Stanley Siebersma
    Navajo, NM
Red Rock Christian Reformed
    Boyd Garnonez
    Box 534, Shiprock, NM 87420
Rehoboth Christian Reformed
    Rolf Veenstra
    Rehoboth, NM 87420

San Antone Christian Reformed
    Alfred Becenti
    Thoreau, NM 87323
Sanostee Christian Reformed
    Frank Curley
    Box 548, Sanostee, NM 87461
Bethel Christian Reformed
    A. W. Koolhaus/Bert Bennally
    Box 10, Shiprock, NM 87420
Teec Nos Pos Christian Reformed
    Paul Redhouse
    Box 1030, Teec Nos Pos, AZ 86514
Toadlena Christian Reformed
    Gary Klumpenhower
    Box 712, Toadlena, NM 87324
Tohatchi Christian Reformed
    Edward Henry
    Box 119, Tohatchi, NM 87325
Toyee Christian Reformed
    Elton Woody
    Box 208, Crownpoint, NM 87313
Tohlakai Christian Reformed
    Mike Harberts
    Star Route 4, Box 20, Gallup, NM 87301
White Horse Lake Christian Reformed
    Howard Begay
    Box 208, Crownpoint, NM 78313
Window Rock Christian Reformed
    Charles Grey
    812 Laguna Circle, Gallup, NM 87301

CHURCH OF CHRIST

Hogback Church of Christ
    C. C. Knose
    Box 196, Waterflow, NM 87421
Kayenta Church of Christ
    Fred Austin
    Box 844, Kayenta, AZ 86033

Montezuma Creek Church of Christ
    P. B. Middlebrook
    Box 220, Montezuma Creek, UT 84534
Navajoland Church of Christ
    J. D. Johnson
    Box 426, Many Farms, AZ 86503
Navajo Church of Christ
    Box 556, Fort Defiance, AZ 86504
Shiprock Church of Christ
    A. B. McPherson
    Box 188, Shiprock, NM 87420
Tuba City Church of Christ
    Don Tullis
    Box 1008, Tuba City, AZ 86045

EPISCOPAL

All Saints Episcopal Church
    Rosella Jim
    Farmington, NM 87401
Good Shepherd Episcopal Church
    Fr. Ned Moore
    Fort Defiance, AZ 86504
St. Anne's Episcopal Church
    Madge Segodi
    Sawmill, AZ 86504
St. Augustine's Episcopal Church
    Uberta Arthur
    Shiprock, NM 87420
St. Christopher's Episcopal Church
    James Sampson
    Bluff, UT 84512
St. Luke's Episcopal Church
    Dr. Lloyd House
    Navajo, AZ
St. Luke's Episcopal Church
    Inez Yazzie
    Carson's Post, NM
St. Mark's Episcopal Church
    Pauline Dick
    Coalmine, AZ

St. Mary's of the Moonlight Episcopal Church
   Oljato, UT
St. Michael's Episcopal Church
   Alice Mason
   Upper Fruitland, NM
San Juan Episcopal Church
   Fr. Henry Bird
   Farmington, NM 87401
San Juan-Batista Episcopal Church
   Fr. Steven Plummer
   Montezuma Creek, UT 84534
Jeddito Camp Church
   Thomas Jackson
   Jeddito, AZ
Many Farms Camp Church
   Thomas Jackson
   Many Farms, AZ 86503

EVANGELICAL LUTHERAN CHURCH

Navajo Evangelical Lutheran Church, Many Farms
   Freddie Garcia
   Many Farms, AZ 86503
Navajo Evangelical Lutheran Church, Navajo
   Donald J. Bren
   Box 1272, Navajo, NM 87328
Navajo Evangelical Lutheran Mission, Rock Point
   Wallace Cole
   Rock Point, Chinle, AZ 86503

FRIENDS

Friends Mission
   Mariano Lake, Thoreau, NM 87323
Rough Rock Friends Mission - Oak Ridge
   Vern Ellis
   Rough Rock, Chinle, AZ 86503
Rough Rock Friends Mission - Rough Rock
   Vern Ellis
   Rough Rock, Chinle, AZ 86503

MENNONITE

Black Mountain Mission - Black Mountain
    Nazwood Burbank
    Chinle, AZ 86503
Black Mountain Mission - Blue Gap
    Peter Burbank
    Chinle, AZ 86503
Church of God in Christ Mennonite
    Wesley Koldn
    Greasewood, AZ 86505
Church of God in Christ Mennonite
    Ervin Jontz
    Box 778, Klagatoh-Wide Ruins, AZ 86502
Church of God in Christ Mennonite
    Jonathan Schmidt
    Salina Springs, Chinle, AZ 86503
Church of God in Christ - Hoghan Hozhoni
    Robert Kachn
    Box 645, Window Rock, AZ 86515

METHODIST

FREE METHODIST
American Indian Mission, Sanostee
    Leo Bennally
    Shiprock, NM 87420
Free Methodist Church
    Burnham, NM
Free Methodist Church
    Toadlena, NM 87324
Free Methodist Church
    Whitehorse Lake, Cuba, NM 87013

UNITED METHODIST
Bisti Methodist Church
    Fred Yazzie
    Box 777, Farmington, NM 87401
First United Methodist Church
    Paul West
    Box 657, Shiprock, NM 87420

Window Rock Methodist
    Box 668, Window Rock, AZ 86515

WESLEYAN COVENANT
Black Hat Mission
    Dennis Gardener
    Window Rock, AZ 86515
Blue Mountain Mission
    G. Evan Freymiller
    Prewitt, NM 87405
Free Trinity Navajo Mission - Gamerco
    Dennis Gardener
    Window Rock, AZ 86515
Indian Holiness Mission
    Carl Noggle
    Box 608, Chambers, AZ 86502
Indian Holiness Mission
    Fruitland, NM 87416
Rock Springs Mission
    Rev. McCormack
    South Hwy. 264, YaTaHey, NM 86515
Wesleyan Holiness
    Karen Gilkinson
    Gallup, NM 87301

MISSION CHURCHES

Alcoholic Rehabilitation Center
    Alan Hill
    Box 172, Ganado, AZ 86505
American Indian Bible Mission
    C. A. Cheesman
    Box 230, Farmington, NM 87401
American Indian Mission
    George Baxter
    2826 N. Petterson, Flagstaff, AZ 86001
Berean Mission - Huerfano Station
    Bloomfield, NM 87413
Berean Mission
    Glenne Marshall
    Box 68, Thoreau, NM 87323

Berean Navajo Church
    Harold Cook
    Box 416, Thoreau, NM 87323
Bisti Camp Camp Church
    Fannie Scott
    Farmington, NM 87401
Coalmine Dzilijiin Church
    Paul Johnson
    Navajo Gospel Mission, Oraibi, AZ 86039
        ...White Grass Church
        ...Forest Lake Church
Crosslands Mission
    Rev. McBride
    Star Route 3, Box 10, Thoreau, NM 87323
Davis, Warren
    Rt. 1, Box 2F, Cortez, CO 81321
Elim Haven
    Mrs. Keist
    Box 66, Continental Divide, NM 87312
Flagstaff Mission to the Navajos
    David Patterson/Kathryn Beard, Directors
    Box AA, Flagstaff, AZ 86001
        ...Flagstaff Indian Bible Church -
            Scott Franklin
        ...Grand Falls Church - James Nataches
        ...Black Falls - Arnold Begay
        ...Gray Mountain - Leslie Cody
        ...Gap Church
        ...Hidden Springs Church
        ...Kayenta Bible Church - Harold Taggart
            Box 332, Kayenta, AZ 86033
Fort Defiance Bible Church
    Tom Kuntz
    Fort Defiance, AZ 86504
Good News Mission
    Iva Lauber
    Box 66, Houck, AZ 86506
Immanuel Mission
    Box 218, Sweetwater, Teec Nos Pos, AZ 86514

Inscription House Navajo Mission
    Bernard Reimer
    Box 50, Tonalea, AZ 86044
    ...Christian Catholic Church
        Amos Grass
        Shonto, AZ
Mentmore Mission
    Ronald J. Endres
    Box 541, Mentmore, NM 87319
Ministry of John 3:16, Inc.
    Robert Kevin
    Box 159, Holbrook, AZ 86025
Navajo Bible School and Mission
    David Clarke, Director
    Box F, Window Rock, AZ 86515
        ...Window Rock Church - Bob Hilderman
        ...Crystal Church - Daniel Taylor
        ...Defiance Church - Louis McCabe
        ...Manuelito Church - Tony Meyers
Navajo Bible Mission
    Chester Dean
    Box 1655, Farmington, NM 87401
Navajo Evangelical Mission
    Tom Siedler
    Hunters Point, St. Michaels, AZ 86511
Navajo Gospel Crusade
    Arthur Norris, Director
    Rt. 1, Box 7, Cortez, CO 81321
        ...Aneth, UT
        ...Montezuma Creek, UT - George Totsonie
Navajo Gospel Mission
    Carlton Lucas, Director
    Box 41, Oraibi, AZ 86039
        ...Pinon - Tom Dolaghan
            Box 446, Pinon, AZ 86510
        ...Whippoorwill - Elsie Begay
        ...Burnt Corn - Jackson Williams
        ...Cactus Valley - James Little
        ...Finger Point - Ed Connover/Goy Begay
Pine Tree Mission
    Earl Whippel
    Star Route 1, Box 7, Gallup, NM 87301

Sand Springs Church
    John McCabe
    Wupatki National Monument, Flagstaff, AZ 86001
Sanders Bible Mission
    Mrs. Wagner
    Box 105, Sanders, AZ 86512
Star Lake Bible Mission
    Claude Fondaw
    Star Route, Cuba, NM 87013
Tsaile Home Church
    Elliot Hogue
    Round Rock Trading Post, Chinle, AZ 86503
Twin Wells Indian School
    Norman Nible
    Box 608, Holbrook, AZ 86025
Whitewater Gospel Mission
    Nora Rady
    Whitewater, NM
Calvary Hogan Mission
    Warren Smith
    Box 945, Chinle, AZ 86503

NAZARENE

Chilchinbito Nazarene Church
    Charley Billie
    Chilchinbito School, Kayenta, AZ 86033
Coppermine Road Nazarene Church
    Alvin Tso
    Box 1177, Page, AZ 86040
Kaibito Nazarene Church
    Johnson Begay
    Kaibito, AZ 86044
Leupp Nazarene Church
    Alex Riggs
    Star Route, Box 76, Winslow, AZ 86047
Montezuma Chair Nazarene Church
    Joseph Curley
    Box 459, Winslow, AZ 86047

Navajo Station Nazarene Church
    Robert Pino
    Box 51, Ganado, AZ 86505
Nazarene Indian Bible School
    Wayne Stark
    2315 Markham Rd., S.W., Albuquerque, NM 87105
Nazarene Indian Mission - Dilkon
    James Paddock
    Star Route, Box 409, Winslow, AZ 86047
Page Nazarene Church
    Alvin Tso
    Box 1177, Page AZ 86040
Pine Hill Nazarene Church
    Robert Pokagon
    Box 6, Ramah, NM 87321
Ramah Onion Nazarene Church
    Johnny Nells
    Box 90, Ramah, NM 87321
Round Cedar Nazarene Church - Leupp
    Rex Tsosie
    Star Route, Box 38, Winslow, AZ 86047
Sand Mountain Nazarene Church
    Sheppie Martine
    Box 184, Ramah, NM 87321
Smoke Signal Nazarene Church
    Lloyd Hughes
    Smoke Signal, Chinle, AZ 86503
Twin Butte Nazarene Mission
    Marshall Keeto
    Box 566, Mentmore, NM 87319
Twin Hills Nazarene Church
    Pete Riggs
    Box 1148, Page, AZ 86040
Window Rock Nazarene Church
    David Scott
    Box 755, Window Rock, AZ 86515
Winslow Nazarene Church
    J. M. Spohn
    1923 W. 2nd Ave., Winslow, AZ 86047

Superintendent: Julian Gunn
                 4229 N. 16th Avenue
                 Phoenix, AZ 85015

PENTECOSTAL

FULL-GOSPEL
Beclabito Full-Gospel Church
   Helen Begay
   Beclabito, Teec Nos Pos, AZ 86514
Bird Springs Full-Gospel Church
   Leonard Curtis
   Star Route, Box 250 Winslow, AZ 86047
Black Mesa Full-Gospel Church
   Junior Yazzie
   Kayenta, AZ 86033
Borrego Pass Full-Gospel Church
   Dan and Amos Barleone
   Borrego Pass, Crownpoint, NM 87313
Cameron Full-Gospel Church
   Thomas Hoover
   Cameron, AZ 86021
Castle Butte House Church
   Gary Taha
   Castle Butte, AZ
Chinle Full-Gospel Church
   Jerry Tom
   Chinle, AZ 86503
Church Rock Full-Gospel Church
   Sister Harvey
   Church Rock, NM 87311
Cottonwood Full-Gospel Church
   Bobby Charlie
   Cottonwood, Chinle, AZ 86503
Dennibito Full-Gospel Church
   Johnny Begodi
Ganado Pentecostal Church
   Tom White
   Ganado, AZ 86505
Gallegos Full-Gospel Church
   Charley Shield
   Gallegos, NM
Kaibito Full-Gospel Church
   Eugene Bennett
   Kaibito, AZ 86044

Lukachukai Full-Gospel Church
    George Davis
    Box 1311, Lukachukai, AZ 86507
Lukachukai Full-Gospel Church
    Margaret Buckingclien
    Lukachukai, AZ 86507
Lupton Camp Church
    Willard Stevens
    Lupton, AZ 86508
Mariano Lake Full-Gospel Church
    Sam Grey
    Thoreau, NM 87323
Mexican Springs Full-Gospel Church
    Emerson Ettsitty
    Mexican Springs, NM 87320
Navajo Full-Gospel Church
    Haswood Brown
    Shiprock, NM 87420
Navajo Nation Christian Center
    Scott Redhouse
    Shiprock, NM 87420
Oak Springs Church
    Russell Jackson
    Red Rock, Shiprock, NM 87420
Pinedale Full-Gospel Church
    Sam Grey
    Thoreau, NM 87323
Red Mesa Full-Gospel Church
    Jack Nakai
    Red Mesa, Teec Nos Pos, AZ 86514
Rock Point Pentecostal Church
    Johnson Bradly
    Rock Point, Chinle, AZ 86503
Sanostee Full-Gospel Church
    George Sanderson
    Sanostee, Shiprock, NM 87420
Sheep Springs Full-Gospel Church
    Alfred Leuppe
    Tohatchi, NM 87325
Shiprock Full-Gospel Church
    Joe Nez
    Shiprock, NM 87420

Sunflower Butte Full-Gospel Church
    Albert Charley
    Indian Wells, AZ 86031
Tseyatoh Camp Church - Phillip Cove
    Louis McCabe
Teec Nos Pos Full-Gospel Church
    Paul Todacheenie
    Teec Nos Pos, AZ 86514
Tinian Full-Gospel Church
    Eddie Castillo
    Cuba, NM 87013
Tonalea Full-Gospel Church
    Homer Bryant
    Tonalea, AZ 86044
Tuba City Full-Gospel Church
    Tuba City, AZ 86045
Twin Lakes Full-Gospel Church
    Charley Johnson
    Twin Lakes, NM
Twin Pines Full-Gospel Church
    Bahe Ettsitty
    Box 53, Counselor, NM 87013
White Post Full-Gospel Church
    Kenneth Begishe
    Shonto, AZ

INDEPENDENT
All Nations Mission
    Mother Renolds
    1102 W. Wilson, Gallup, NM 87301
Aneth Pentecostal Church
    Johnny Billie
    Aneth, UT 84510
Bisti Pentecostal Church
    Charley Shield
    Farmington, NM 87401
Bisti Home Church
    Harvey K'aai
    Farmington, NM 87401
Castle Butte Navajo Indian Mission
    Ross Vernon Mericle
    Box 296, Holbrook, AZ 86025

Christian Revival Fellowship
    M. G. Wooten
    Box 362, Cortez, CO 81321
De Deez Ahi Church
    Carlos Moore
    White Cone, Indian Wells, AZ 86031
Defiance Pentecostal Church
    Sam Joe Spenser
    Defiance, Manuelito, NM
Desert View Mission
    Sister Janson
    Box 1814, Farmington, NM 87401
Gallup Independent Pentecostal Church
    Doris Alger
    700 N. Russian Street, Gallup, NM 87301
Greasewood Pentecostal Church
    Ben James
    Greasewood, AZ 86505
Harvest-Time Mission - Sun Valley Station
    Holbrook, AZ 86025
Haystack Mission
    Sister Lee
    Prewitt, NM 87045
Holiness Indian Mission
    Brother Poppelwells
    Church Rock, NM 87311
        ...Blue Water Outstation
Many Farms House Church
    Kii Begay
    Many Farms, AZ 86503
Miracle Church
    Blanco, NM 87412
Miracle Revival Church
    Don Ellison
    Red Rock, Shiprock, NM 87420
Navajo Mission Pentecostal Holiness Church
    McElvie Purifoy
    Greasewood Boarding School, Ganado, AZ 86505
Navajo Trails Tabernacle
    George Hanson
    Box 743, Flagstaff, AZ 86001

New Testament Church
    Joe Nakai
    Red Rock, Shiprock, NM 87420
Ninety & Nine Indian Mission
    Eddie Garver
    Hwy. 99, Star Route, Winslow, AZ 86041
Oljeto Pentecostal Church
    Harry Sanders
    Oljeto, Monument Valley, UT 84536
Oral Roberts Church
    Tom Nelson
    Black Hat, Window Rock, AZ 86515
Red Rock Pentecostal Church
    Terry Goodwin
    612 S. 7th, Gallup, NM 87301
Smith Lake Pentecostal Church
    Sister Tate
    Thoreau, NM 87323
The Door (Four-Square)
    Ernie Lister
    400 N. 2nd Street, Gallup, NM 87301
Thoreau Revival Center
    Russell P. Barker
    Manuelito, NM 87318
Tinian Pentecostal Church
    James Toledo
    Cuba, NM 87013
Tohlakai Pentecostal Church
    Joseph Curman
    Tohlakai, Gallup, NM 87301
Waterflow Pentecostal Mission
    Waterflow, NM 87421

PENTECOSTAL CHURCH OF GOD
Bread Springs Pentecostal Church of God
    Harry John
    Bread Springs, Gallup, NM 87301
Church of God Indian Mission
    Denzel Teague
    Box 757, Gallup, NM 87301

Gallup Pentecostal Church of God
    John Hubbard
    634 N. 11th, Gallup, NM 87301
Houck Pentecostal Church of God
    Hoskie Joe
    Houck, AZ 86506
Kayenta Pentecostal Church of God
    Johnny Thompson
    Kayenta, AZ 86033
Kit Carson Cave Pentecostal Church of God
    Sister Whitman
    Church Rock, NM 87311
Kit Carson Cave Pentecostal Church of God
    Sam Giegos
    Church Rock, NM 87311
Klagatoh Pentecostal Church of God
    Bahe Woodman
    Klagatoh, Cambers, AZ 86502
Mountain View Pentecostal Church of God
    Pauline Pafilita
    Ramah, NM 87321
Neesjaa Pentecostal Church of God
    Shep D. Martine
    Ramah, NM 87321
Pentecostal Church of God of America
    Sister Tobeck
    Thoreau, NM 87323
Peria Pentecostal Church of God
    Buddie Clarke, District Overseer
    Ft. Wingate, NM 87316
Pinedale Pentecostal Church of God
    Kenneth Begay
    Church Rock, NM 87311
Red Lake Pentecostal Church of God
    Carol Irwin/Marcell Kennedy
    Box 713, Winslow, AZ 86047
Rocky Point Pentecostal Church of God
    Tom Chischilli
    Box 215, Mentmore, NM 87319
Sand Mountain Pentecostal Church of God
    Shep D. Martine
    Ramah, NM 87321

Valley View Pentecostal Church of God
    Harry Begay
    Valley View, Gallup, NM 87301
Winslow Pentecostal Church of God
    Edgar L. Haskinson
    Alder and First Streets, Winslow, AZ 86047

UNITED PENTECOSTAL
Gallup United Pentecostal Church
    Sister Eastridge
    Gallup, NM 87301
Newcomb United Pentecostal Church
    Jerry Eastridge
    Tohatchi, NM 87325
Tohatchi United Pentecostal Church
    Jerry Eastridge
    Tohatchi, NM 87325

WORD OF GOD CHURCH
Lighthouse Mission
    Isabel and Joe Salazar
    Star Lake, Cuba, NM 87013
Word of God Church - Rincon Marquis
    Philip Apatchito
    Cuba, NM 87013
Word of God Church - Sanostee Full-Gospel
    Edith Smiley
    Sanostee, Shiprock, NM 87420
Word of God Church - Sweetwater
    Willis George
    Teec Nos Pos, AZ 86514
Word of God Church - White Horse Lake
    Betty and Earl Betone
    Cuba, NM 87013

PRESBYTERIAN

Chinle Presbyterian Church
    Rev. Richard Lupke/Jimmy Tsosie
    Chinle, AZ 86503

Del Muerto Presbyterian Church
    Jimmy Tsosie
    Chinle, AZ 86503
Denehotsoh Presbyterian Church
    Woody Yazzie
    Kayenta, AZ 86033
Ganado Presbyterian Church
    Rev. James Vandyke
    Ganado, AZ 86505
Indian Wells Presbyterian Church
    Box 2, Indian Wells, AZ 86031
Kaibito Presbyterian Church
    Lester Dzil
    Kaibito, AZ 86044
Kayenta Presbyterian Church
    Rev. David Morelli
    Box 277, Kayenta, AZ 86033
Leupp Presbyterian Church
    Rev. Johnny Cooke
    Leupp, AZ 86035
Nazlini Presbyterian Church
    Rev. Richard Lupke/Jimmy Tsosie
    Chinle, AZ 86503
Oljeto Presbyterian Church
    Cecil Todicheenee
    Kayenta, AZ 86033
Tuba City Presbyterian Church
    Rev. Harold Borhauer
    Tuba City, AZ 86045

SEVENTH DAY ADVENTIST

Lavida Mission
    Leroy Moore
    Box 1289, Farmington, NM 87401
Chinle Seventh Day Adventist Church
    Letha Meyer
    146-2 Apache Street, Box 1, Chinle, AZ 86503
Holbrook Seventh Day Adventist Church
    Berton Wright
    Box 880, Holbrook, AZ 86025
Monument Valley Seventh Day Adventist Church
    Goulding's Trading Post, Mexican Hat, UT

Bibliography

ABERLE, DAVID
    1966   The Peyote Religion Among the Navajo. Chicago, Aldine Publishing Co.

ADAMS, WILLIAM Y.
    1971   " Navajo Social Organization " American Anthropologist 73 273

ALBERT, E. M.
    1956   "The Classification of Values" American Anthropologist 58 221-248

ALLEN, ROLAND
    1964   Missionary Methods: St. Paul's or Ours? Grand Rapids, Eerdmans

    1967   The Spontaneous Expansion of the Church. Grand Rapids, Eerdmans

BEAVER, R. PIERCE
    1966   Church, State, and the American Indians. St. Louis, Mo., Concordia Publishing House

BINGHAM, SAM AND JANET
    1976   Navajo Chapter Government Handbook. Rock Point, Ariz., Rock Point Community School

BRUGGE, DAVID M.
    1968   Navajos in the Catholic Church Records of New Mexico 1694-1785. Research Reports 16, 160 Window Rock, Ariz., Navajo Tribe

BULOW, ERNEST L.
    1972   Navajo Taboos. Window Rock, Ariz., Navajo Times Publishing Company

COLLIER, JOHN
    1967   "The Navajos" Anthropology, Rapport and Wright, eds. New York, New York University Press 297-318

COLLIER, M. C.
    1946   "Leadership at Navajo Mountain and Klage-
            toh" American Anthropologist 48 137-138

    1966   Local Organization Among the Navajo. New
            Haven, Conn., Human Relations Area Files,
            Inc.

DE KORNE, J. C.
    1947   Navajo and Zuni for Christ. Grand Rapids,
            Christian Reformed Board of Missions

DELORIA, VINE, JR.
    1969   Custer Died for Your Sins: An Indian Man-
            ifesto. New York, Avon Books

d'EPINAY, C. LALIVE
    1967   "The Training of Pastors and Theological
            Education: The Case of Chile" Internation-
            al Review of Missions 56 185-192

DITTMANN, A. T. AND H. C. MOORE
    1957   "Disturbance in Dreams as Related to Peyo-
            tism Among the Navajo" American Anthropol-
            ogist 59 642-649

DOWNS, JAMES F.
    1972   The Navajo. New York, Holt, Rinehart and
            Winston

DUTTON, BERTHA P.
    1975   Navajos and Apaches: The Athabascan Peo-
            ples. Englewood Cliffs, New Jersey, Pren-
            tice Hall Inc.

DYK, WALTER
    1938   Son of Old Man Hat. (Paperback edition
            1966 Lincoln, Univ. of Nebraska Press)

ENGEL, JAMES F. AND WILBERT H. NORTON
    1975   What's Gone Wrong With the Harvest? Grand
            Rapids, Eerdmans

1976   "Church Growth Strategies Plus" Evangelical Missions Quarterly Vol. 12 #2

FERGUSON, F. N.
1968   "Navajo Drinking: Some Tentative Hypothesis" Human Organization 27 159-167

FOSTER, GEORGE M.
1962   Traditional Cultures, and the Impact of
Technological Change. New York, Harper and
Bros.

FRANCISCAN FATHERS OF ST. MICHAELS
An Ethnologic Dictionary of the Navajo
Language. St. Michaels, Ariz., St. Mi-
chael's Press

GERBER, VERGIL
1973   God's Way to Keep a Church Going and Growing. Pasadena, Ca., William Carey Library

GRAVES, THEOLORE D.
1967   "Acculteration, Access, and Alcohol in a
Tri-ethnic Community" American Anthropologist 69 306-321

1970   "The Personal Adjustmant of Navajo Indian
Migrants to Denver, Colo." American Anthropologist 23 337-350

HAILE, B.
1935   "Religious Concepts of the Navajo Indians"
Catholic Philosophical Assoc., Proceedings
10 84-98

1949   "Emergence Myth According to the Hanalth-
maye or Upward Reaching Rite" Navajo Religion Series 3 1-186

1954   "Property Concepts of the Navajo Indians "
Anthropological Series, Catholic University of America 17 1-64

HAMMOND, BLODWEN AND MARY SHEPARDSON
    1965   "The 'born-between' Phenomenon Among the
            Navajo" American Anthropologist 67 1516-
            1517

HODGE, WILLIAM H.
    1964   "Navajo Pentecostalism" Anthropological
            Quarterly Vol. 37, No. 3 73-93

    1969   The Albuquerque Navajos. Tucson,University
            of Arizona Press

HODGES, MELVIN L.
    1965   " Developing Basic Units of Indigenous
            Churches" Church Growth and Christian Mis-
            sion,edit. by Donald A. McGavran,New York,
            Harper and Row

    1972   "Are Indigenous Church Principles Out-
            dated?" Evangelical Missions Quarterly 9
            (Fall) 43-46

    1973   A Guide to Church Planting. Chicago, Moody
            Press

JOHNSTON, BERNICE
    1972   "Two Ways in the Desert: A Study of Modern
            Navajo-Anglo Relations" Pasadena, Socio-
            Technical Publications 12 334

KELLY, LAWRENCE
    1970   Navajo Roundup. Boulder, Colo., Pruett

KELLY, ROGER E. AND JOHN CRAMER
    1966   "American Indians in Small Cities:A Survey
            of Urban Acculturation in Two Northern
            Arizona Communities" Northern Ariz. Uni-
            versity, Dept. of Rehabilitation, 1-90

KLUCKHOHN, C. AND D. LEIGHTON
    1946   The Navajo. Cambridge, Harvard Univ. Press

    1961   "The Navajo View of Life" The Fate of Man,
            C.C. Brinton, ed. New York, George Brazil-
            ler 37-44

KLUCKHOHN, CLYDE
    1962   <u>Navajo Witchcraft.</u> (Paperback edition, 3rd printing 1970) Boston, Beacon Press

    1969   <u>Mirror for Man: The Relation of Anthropology to Modern Life.</u> New York, Whittlesey House

KRAFT, CHARLES H.
    1963a   "Christian Conversion or Cultural Conversion?" <u>Practical Anthropology</u> 10 179-187

LaBARRE, WESTON
    1959   <u>The Peyote Cult.</u> Hamden, The Shoestring Press (Enlarged paperback edition, New York, Schocken Books)

LEIGHTON, D. AND CLYDE KLUCKHOHN
    1969   <u>Children of the People (Navajo).</u> New York, Octagon Books (First published 1947)

LESSA, WILLIAM A. AND EVON Z. VOGT
    1965   <u>Reader in Comparative Religion: An Anthropological Approach(3rd edition).</u> New York, Harper and Row

LOEWEN, JACOB A.
    1966   "The Question of the Communication of the Gospel" Practical Anthropology 13 213-226

    1968   "Why Minority Languages Persist or Die" <u>Practical Anthropology</u> 15 8-15

    1975   <u>Culture and Human Values: Christian Intervention in Anthropological Perspective.</u> South Pasadena. William Carey Library

LUCKERT, KARL
    1975   <u>The Navajo Hunter Tradition.</u> Tucson, Univ. of Arizona Press

LUABETAK, LOUIS J.
    1970   <u>The Church and Cultures: An Applied Anthropology for the Religious Worker.</u> South Pasadena, William Carey Library

MALEHORN, PAULINE
    1948   The Tender Plant. Farmington, New Mexico,
            Navajo Methodist Mission

MALINOWSKI, BRONISLAW
    1948   Magic, Science and Religion. New York,
            Doubleday and Co.

MARRIOTT, ALICE AND CAROL K. RACHLIN
    1971   Peyote. New York, New American Library

MATTHEWS, WASHINGTON
    1883   "A Part of the Navajos Mythology" American
            Antiquarian and Oriental Journal 5 207-
            224

    1886   "Some Deities and Demons of the Navajo"
            American Naturalist 20 841-850

McGAVRAN, DONALD A.
    1955   The Bridges of God. New York, Friendship

    1959   How Churches Grow. New York, Friendship

    1970   Understanding Church Growth. Grand Rapids,
            Eerdmans

    1972   Crucial Issues in Missions Tomorrow. Chi-
            cago, Moody

MEANS, FLORENCE C.
    1955   Sagebrush Surgeon. New York, Friendship
            Press

MORGAN, W.
    1931   "Navajo Treatment of Sickness" American
            Anthropologist 33 390-402

NEVIUS, JOHN
    1958   Planting and Development of Missionary
            Churches. Philadelphia, Presbyterian and
            Reformed Publishing Co.

NEWCOMB, FRANC
 1964 Hosteen Klah, Navajo Medicine Man and Sand
    Painter. Norman, University of Oklahoma
    Press

 1966 Navaho Neighbors. Norman, University of
    Oklahoma Press

NIDA, EUGENE
 1954 Customs and Cultures. South Pasadena, Wil-
    liam Carey Library

 1960 Message and Mission: The Communication of
    the Christian Faith. South Pasadena, Wil-
    liam Carey Library

 1965 "Culture and Church Growth" Practical An-
    thropology 12 22-37

OPPENHUIZEN, ED AND JOHN KLEIN
 n.d. "A Brief Introduction to New Workers on
    the Indian Mission Field" unpublished
    manuscript

ORTIZ, JUAN CARLOS
 1975 Call to Discipleship. Plainfield, N.J.,
    Logos International

RAYMOND, FRIDAY LOCKE
 1976 The Book of the Navajo. Los Angeles, Man-
    kind Publishing Co.

REICHARD, GLADYS A.
 1941 "The Navajo and Christianity" American An-
    thropologist 51 66-71

 1945 "Distinctive Features of the Navajo Reli-
    gion" Southwestern Journal of Anthropolo-
    gy, Albuquerque, N. Mexico 1 199-200

 1963 Navajo Religion: A Study of Symbolism. New
    York, Pantheon Books

ROESSEL, RUTH, ed.
    1971   Navajo Studies at Navajo Community Col-
            lege. Many Farms, Ariz., Navajo Community
            College Press

    1973   Navajo Stories of the Long Walk Period.
            Tsaile Campus, Chinle, Ariz., Navajo Com-
            munity College Press

SALSBURY, CORA B.
    n.d.   Forty Years in the Desert; A History of
            Ganado Mission 1901-1940. Ganado, Ariz.

SHEPARDSON, MARY AND BLODWEN HAMMOND
    1970   The Navajo Mountain Community. Berkeley,
            University of California Press

SLOTKIN, J. S.
    1955   "Peyotism, 1521-1891" American Anthropolo-
            gist 57   202-230

SMALLEY, WILLIAM A.
    1958   "Cultural Implications of an Indigenous
            Church" Practical Anthropology 5 51 -65

    1959   "What are Indigenous Churches Like?" Prac-
            tical Anthropology 6   135-139

    1967   Readings in Missionary Anthropology, ed.
            South Pasadena, William Carey Library

SMITH, RICHARD K. AND NELSON J. MELVIN
    1969   Datelines and Bylines: A Sketchbook of
            Presbyterian and Growth in Arizona. Synod
            of Arizona

SPENCER, KATHERINE
    1957   Mythology and Values. (An Analysis of Nav-
            ajo Chantway Myths) Philadelphia, American
            Folklore Society

SPICER, EDWARD H.
    1961   Perspectives in American Indian Culture
            Change. Chicago, Univ. of Chicago Press

STEINER, STAN
   1968   The New Indians. New York, Dell Publ. Co.

TERRELL, JOHN UPTON
   1972   The Navajos. New York, Harper and Row

TIPPETT, ALAN R.
   1962   "Ethnic Cohesion and Intra-configurational Involvement in the Acceptance of Cultural Change in Indonesia" Acceptance and Rejection of Christianity, unpublished bound manuscript,School of World Mission, Fuller Theological Seminary, Pasadena, Ca.

   1963   "Initiation Rites and Functional Substitutes" Practical Anthropology 12 85-91

   1967b   Solomon Islands Christianity: A Study in Growth and Obstruction. South Pasadena, William Carey Library

   1969   Verdict Theology in Missionary Theory. Lincoln, Ill. Lincoln Christian College Press (publ. 1973 South Pasadena, William Carey Library)

   1970a   Church Growth and the Word of God: The Biblical Basis of the Church Growth Viewpoint. Grand Rapids, Eerdmans

   1971b   "Patterns of Religious Change in Communal Society" Adventures in Missiology, Manus. awaiting publication (chapter duplicated for class use

   1973   God, Man and Church Growth, ed. Grand Rapids, Eerdmans

UNDERHILL, RUTH
   1956   The Navajos. Norman, Univ. of Oklahoma Press

WAGNER, C. PETER
    1971   Frontiers in Missionary Strategy. Chicago,
                Moody Press

    1973   Look Out! The Pentecostals Are Coming.
                Carol Stream, Ill., Creation House

    1974   Stop the World I Want to Get On. Glendale,
                Regal Books

WALLACE, A. F. C.
    1956   "Revitalization Movements" American An-
                thropologist 58 264-281

WARNER, MICHAEL J.
    1970   "Protestant Missionary Activity Among the
                Navajo, 1890-1912" New Mexico Historical
                Review 45 209-232

WINTER, RALPH D.
    1970   The Twenty-Five Unbelievable Years 1945-
                1969. South Pasadena,William Carey Library

YAZZIE, DOLLIE L.
    1976   Navajo Music. (For classroom enrichment)
                Rough Rock, Az., Navajo Curriculum Center

YAZZIE, ETHELOU, ed.
    1971   Navajo History. Many Farms, Ariz., Navajo
                Community College Press

YOUNG, ROBERT AND WILLIAM MORGAN
    1954   Navajo Historical Selections. Phoenix,
                Phoenix Indian School Print Shop

YOUNG, ROBERT
    1968   The Role of the Navajo in the Southwestern
                Drama. Gallup, N. Mexico, The Gallup Inde-
                pendent

DAVID SCATES has served as a missionary to the Navajo
Indians for twelve years under the auspices of the Navajo
Christian Churches. A native of Colorado, he is currently
residing there in Dolores doing field research.

THOMAS DOLAGHAN is presently Director of Church Development with the Navajo Gospel Mission in Pinon, Arizona,
where he has worked in the areas of church planting and
evangelism for the past fifteen years.

Recent study of the authors at the School of World Mission at Fuller Theological Seminary in Pasadena, California stimulated the research which is the subject of this
book.

BOOKS BY WILLIAM CAREY LIBRARY

STRATEGY OF MISSION

Church Growth and Christian Mission by Donald A. McGavran, $4.95x paper, 256 pp.

Committed Communities: Fresh Streams for World Missions by Charles J. Mellis, $3.95 paper, 160 pp.

The Conciliar-Evangelical Debate: The Crucial Documents, 1964-1976 edited by Donald McGavran, $8.95 paper, 400 pp.

Crucial Dimensions in World Evangelization edited by Arthur F. Glasser et al., $7.95x paper, 480 pp.

Evangelical Missions Tomorrow edited by Wade T. Coggins and Edwin L. Frizen, Jr., $5.95 paper, 208 pp.

The Grounds for a New Thrust in World Mission by Ralph D. Winter, $.75 booklet, 32 pp.

Here's How: Health Education by Extension by Ronald and Edith Seaton, $3.45 paper, 144 pp.

The Indigenous Church and the Missionary by Melvin L. Hodges, $2.95 paper, 108 pp.

A Manual for Church Growth Surveys by Ebbie C. Smith, $3.95 paper, 144 pp.

Mission: A Practical Approach to Church-Sponsored Mission Work by Daniel C. Hardin, $4.95x paper, 264 pp.

Readings in Third World Missions: A Collection of Essential Documents edited by Marlin L. Nelson, $6.95x paper, 304 pp.

Social Action vs. Evangelism: An Essay on the Contemporary Crisis by William J. Richardson, $1.95x paper, 64 pp.

The 25 Unbelievable Years: 1945-1969 by Ralph D. Winter, $2.95 paper, 128 pp.

The Word-Carrying Giant: The Growth of the American Bible Society by Creighton Lacy, $5.95 paper, 320 pp.

APPLIED ANTHROPOLOGY

Becoming Bilingual: A Guide to Language Learning by Donald Larson and William A. Smalley, $5.95x paper, 426 pp.

Christopaganism or Indigenous Christianity? edited by Tetsunao Yamamori and Charles R. Taber, $5.95 paper, 242 pp.

The Church and Cultures: Applied Anthropology for the Religious Worker by Louis J. Luzbetak, $5.95x paper, 448 pp.

Culture and Human Values: Christian Intervention in Anthropological Perspective (writings of Jacob Loewen) edited by William A. Smalley, $5.95x paper, 466 pp.

Customs and Cultures: Anthropology for Christian Missions by Eugene A. Nida, $3.95 paper, 322 pp.

Manual of Articulatory Phonetics by William A. Smalley, $5.95x paper, 522 pp.

Message and Mission: The Communication of the Christian Faith by Eugene A. Nida, $3.95x paper, 254 pp.

Readings in Missionary Anthropology edited by William A. Smalley, $5.95x paper, 384 pp.

Tips on Taping: Language Recording in the Social Sciences by Wayne and Lonna Dickerson, $4.95x paper, 208 pp.